Canon EOS R50 Instructional Handbook

A User-friendly Guidebook Tailored to Assist R50 Owners in Mastering their Camera's Features

By

Harry Bass

Table of Contents

INTRODUCTION

The Canon EOS R50 is a compact and light mirrorless camera perfect for capturing photos and videos. It has improved features compared to its predecessor, the EOS M50 Mark II, making it suitable for vloggers and creative enthusiasts.

The R50 camera has a powerful 24.2MP sensor and advanced image processors that create sharp and vibrant photos. It works well in different lighting conditions with an ISO range of 100-32,000 (extendable to 51200). It can shoot slow-motion videos in Full HD 1080 at 120 frames per second and record high-quality 6K oversampled UHD 4K videos at 30 frames per second. Thanks to its DIGIC X processor, the camera's electronic shutter allows fast, continuous shooting at 15 frames per second for action shots and smooth 4K footage.

The R50 has a cool Dual Pixel CMOS AF II feature with 651 autofocus zones. It helps the camera focus quickly and accurately. This tech can recognize people, animals, and cars, keeping them in sharp focus in photos and videos. It's convenient for vloggers and video makers who want smooth and reliable autofocus tracking.

The R50 camera has a large 3.0-inch touchscreen that's easy to use for adjusting focus, navigating menus, and reviewing photos. It also comes with a sharp electronic viewfinder for a great experience. The screen can be tilted for comfortable use at different angles. The Advanced A+ Assist feature helps capture excellent photos, even in challenging situations like night scenes and backlighting. It automatically controls overexposure and takes multiple continuous shots to produce stunning nighttime and macro photos with better focus.

The R50 camera can shoot explicit 4K videos without cutting off any part of the image, record high-speed Full-HD videos at 120 frames per second, and has a special mode for vlogging and making videos. This mode is great for showing products in tutorials, like makeup or cooking videos, as it quickly shifts focus from the person on camera to an item held up to the lens. Plus, you can continuously record videos for up to an hour, making it easy to create content for your vlog, podcast, or other projects without interruptions.

The R50 camera lets you quickly transfer photos and videos with wired and wireless options. You can connect it to smart devices using Bluetooth through the Canon Camera Connect app. It also has a USB-C port, micro-HDMI port, and microphone input for video recording. The built-in Wi-Fi allows smooth operations like remote live viewing and file transfer. Plus, the R50 can be used as a web camera for streaming Full HD video without extra software, making it great for online content creators.

CHAPTER 1: GETTING THE CAMERA UP AND RUNNING

Preparing the Camera for Initial Use

Charging the Battery

1. Remove the protective cover from the battery.

2. Attach the battery to the adapter completely.

3. Charge the battery using the LC-E17 charger:

    - Plug the charger into a wall outlet.

    - Connect the power cable to the charger.

    - The charging starts automatically; the indicator turns orange and changes to green when fully charged.

    - It takes about two hours at normal temperatures, but charging may vary based on temperature and remaining battery capacity.

    - Charging in low temperatures may take longer (5-10°C/41-50°F).

    - Charge the battery the day before or the day you use it.

    - Charged batteries lose power over time, even when not in use.

9

- Once charged, remove the battery and unplug the charger.

How to insert the battery and card

1. Insert a fully charged card and Battery Pack LP-E17 into the camera. The card saves the photos you take.

2. Unlock the card/battery compartment cover and put in the battery. Make sure to attach the end with the electrical contacts.

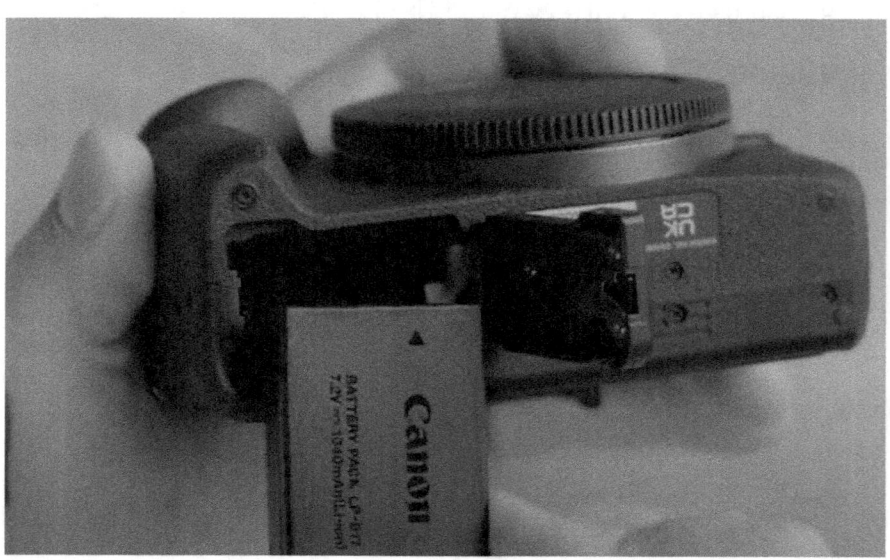

3. Insert the card into the slot with the label facing the front of the camera until it clicks into place.

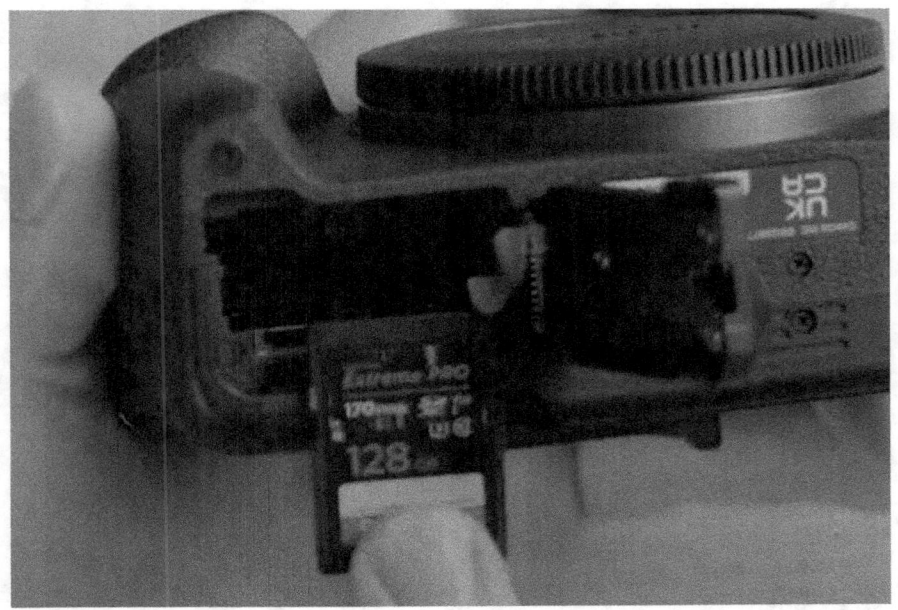

4. Close the lid securely. Slide the card/battery compartment cover lock to lock it after pressing the cover shut.

How to remove the card

Use this camera to set up the card if it's new or another camera or computer has already formatted it.

1. Open the cover of the card/battery compartment.

2. Remove the battery by pushing the battery lock lever, and keep the protective cover on it.

3. Gently push the card to eject it, and remember to close the lid after removing it.

Attaching/Detaching a Lens

Attaching a Lens

1. Remove the caps by twisting off the body cap and rear lens cap.

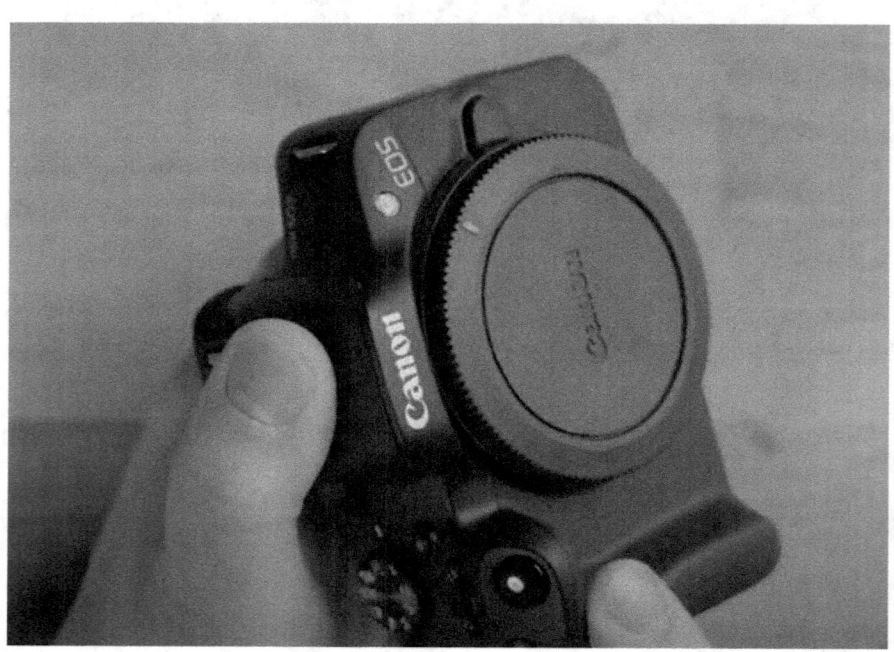

2. Attach the lens.

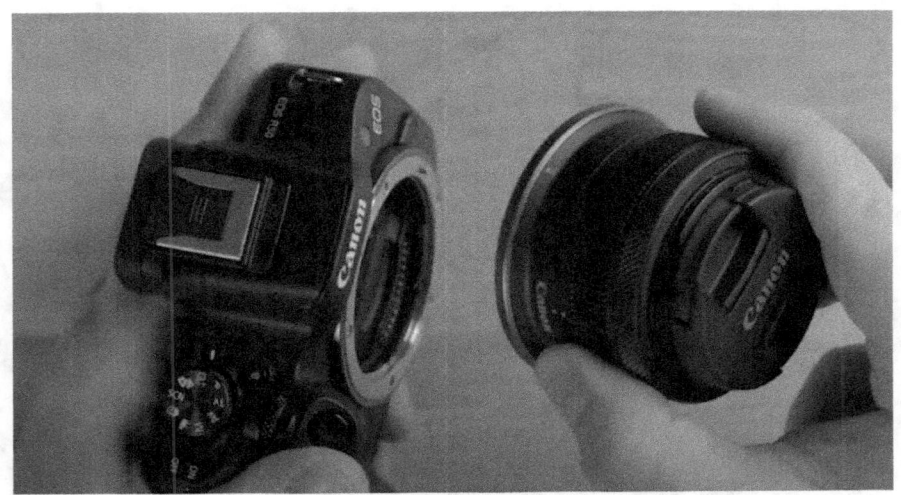

3. Choose autofocus (<AF>) as the focus mode. Remember, <AF> stands for autofocus, and <MF> for manual focus. Turn on autofocus in the focus mode settings.

Detaching a Lens

1. Twist the adapter following the arrow and press the lens release button to remove the lens. Keep turning until it stops.

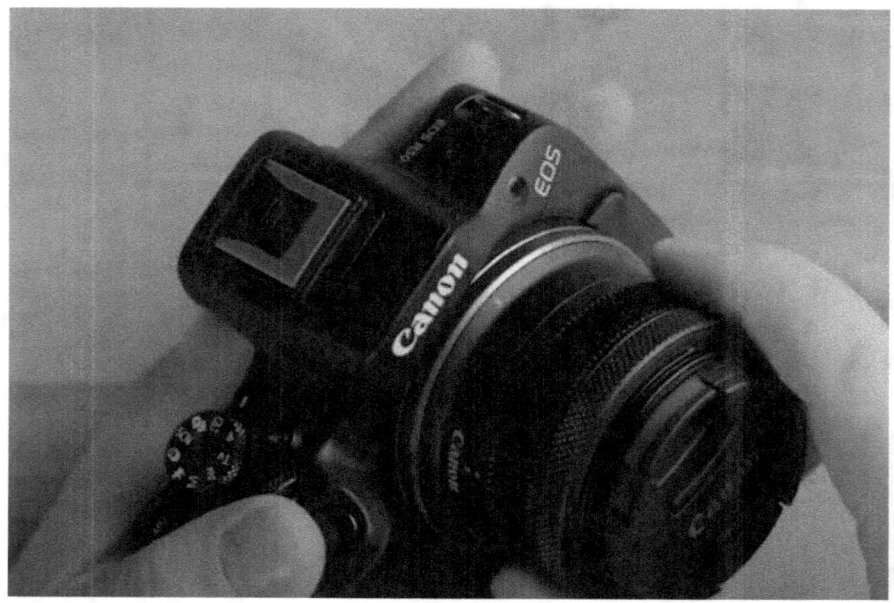

2. Remove the lens from the adapter by turning it counterclockwise while pressing the lens release lever.

How to Change a Menu Setting

To change a menu setting on the Canon EOS R50, do these steps:

1. Press "Menu" on the camera or touch the "Menu" symbol on the screen to open the menu.

2. Use the touch screen or navigation buttons to find the category with your desired setting.

3. Once you locate the option, press or highlight it with navigation buttons.

4. Adjust the setting to your preference using the navigation buttons or touch screen.

5. Click "Set" to save changes and exit the menu.

Note: Finding specific settings might involve exploring sub-menus. Some settings may have limited options or be unavailable based on camera settings or circumstances.

Using the Quick Control Settings

You can easily and quickly access the common camera settings using the Canon EOS R50's Quick Control Screen.

Here's how to use the Quick Control Screen:

1. Tap the "Q" button on the camera screen.

2. Look at the Quick Control Screen on the LCD.

3. Use buttons or a touch screen to pick a setting.

4. Change the value using touch or buttons.

5. Press "Set" to confirm and return to shooting mode after adjusting.

The Quick Control Screen displays different settings based on camera mode and shooting choices. Manual mode shows options like aperture, shutter speed, ISO, and exposure compensation. In other modes, it may show settings for shooting modes, aspect ratios, or other options.

You can change the Quick Control Screen to display only the settings you use often. Go to the camera's main menu, choose Custom Controls, and assign your favorite settings to the custom function buttons. Now, when you press those buttons, your settings will appear on the Quick Control Screen.

Exploring External Camera Features

Topside controls

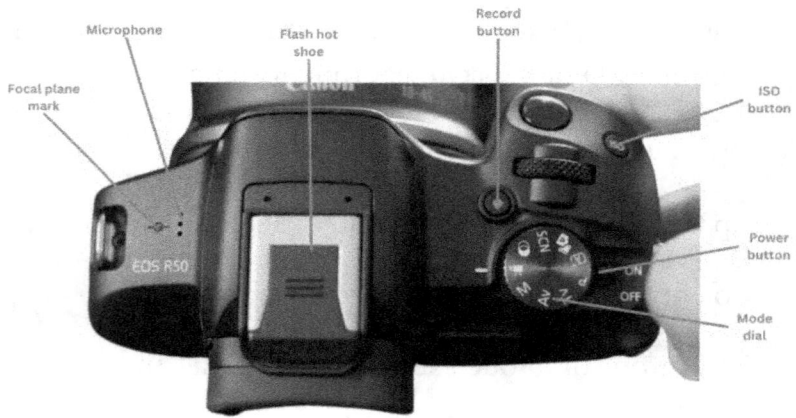

- **Mode Dial:** Choose various shooting modes, including Auto, Creative (P, Av, Tv, M), Movie, Scene Modes, and more.

- **Power Switch:** Turns the camera on and off.

- **Multi-Function Button:** Accesses quick settings like image size, focus area, drive mode, and white balance.

16

- **Flash Hot Shoe:** Connects external flash units for additional lighting in low-light situations.

- **Microphone:** It has a built-in stereo microphone located on the top of the camera, just behind the hot shoe. This microphone is suitable for capturing basic audio in everyday situations, but it may not be sufficient for professional or demanding video projects.

- **Shutter Release Button:** Captures photographs or starts/stops video recording.

- **Main Command Dial:** Adjusts exposure settings like aperture (in Av mode), shutter speed (in Tv mode), and ISO in all modes.

- **Exposure Compensation Button:** Adjusts overall image brightness by +/-3 stops in increments of 1/3 stop.

- **Focal Plane Mark:** It indicates the position of the image sensor inside the camera. This mark is primarily useful for precise distance measurements or when using certain specialized techniques like macro photography.

- **Record Button:** Starts and stops video recording.

- **Movie Mode/Still Mode Switch:** Toggles between still photography and video recording modes.

- **Customizable Buttons:** Two buttons near the shutter release for frequently used functions like white balance, AF selection, or image review.

Front features

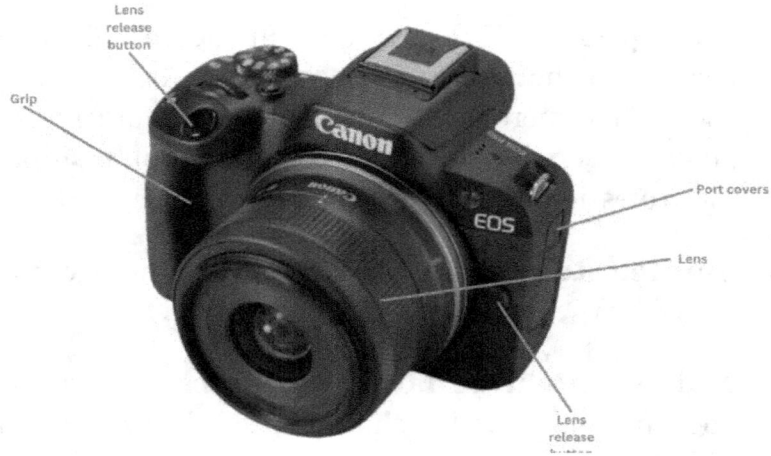

1. **Lens Mount:** Attaches your lens to the camera body, channeling light and forming the image you capture.

2. **Lens Release Button:** Detaches the lens from the camera body for lens changes or sensor cleaning.

3. **Focus Assist Lamp:** Helps the autofocus system lock onto your subject in low-light situations.

4. **AF Assist Button:** Temporarily illuminates the subject with a flash to assist autofocus in dim environments.

5. **Control Ring:** Located on some lenses, allows you to control aperture, shutter speed, or other settings directly with your fingers.

6. **Grip:** Where you place your hand while holding the camera.

7. **Port covers:** Houses the different ports.

Back-of-the-body controls

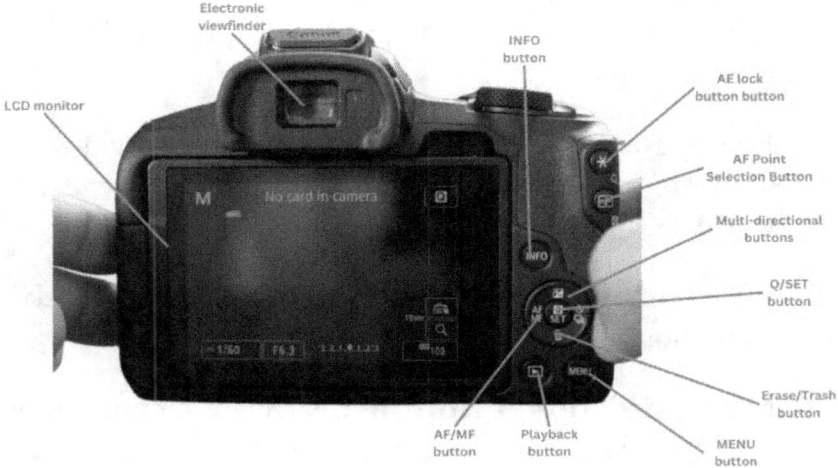

1. **Electronic Viewfinder (EVF):** Peek through this digital window to see your composition and adjust settings before capturing the moment.

2. **LCD touchscreen:** This touch-sensitive screen lets you review photos, navigate menus, choose focus points, and even zoom in for precise adjustments.

3. **AF Point Selection Button:** Choose where you want the camera to focus using the joystick or touch the desired point on the screen.

4. **Menu Button:** Dive into the world of settings to customize your shooting experience and unlock the camera's full potential.

5. **INFO Button:** Toggle various on-screen displays like the histogram, gridlines, and shooting information for greater control.

6. **Playback Button:** Review your captured photos and videos, zoom in for details, and even delete the unwanted ones.

7. **Erase Button:** Send unwanted photos or videos to oblivion (remember, there's no "undo" in the digital world!).

8. **SET Button:** Confirm your menu selections and lock in your chosen settings.

9. **Multi-directional Buttons:** Navigate menus, adjust values, and select options using these handy buttons.

10. **Q (Quick Menu) Button:** Access frequently used settings like image size, drive mode, and white balance with a quick tap.

11. **AE lock button:** It allows you to lock the current exposure settings (aperture, shutter speed, and ISO) selected by the camera's light meter.

Working with Memory Cards

You can try out the basic controls I explained by clearing a memory card. There are three ways to make a blank memory card for your camera, but two are only partially right. Your choices include both correct and incorrect options.

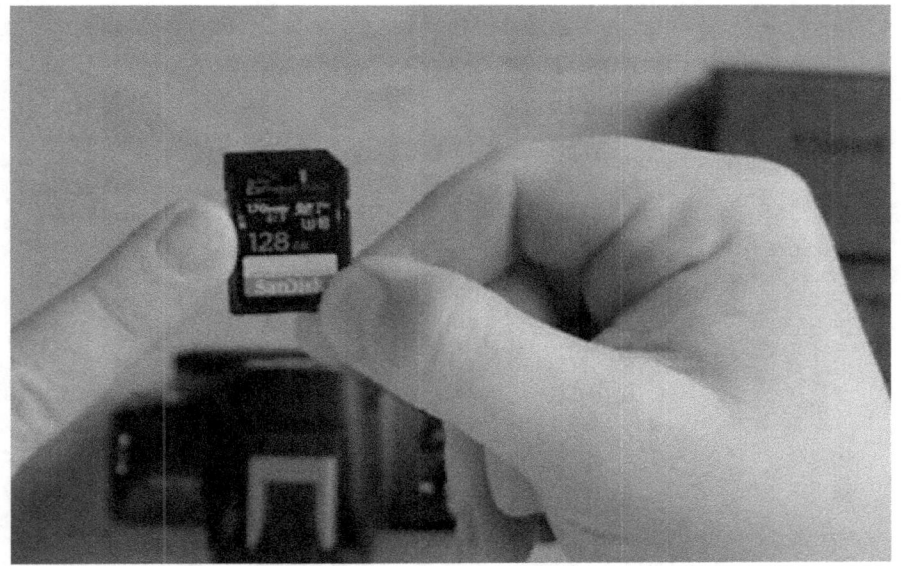

- **Transfer (move) files to your computer:** When you move all your pictures from the camera's memory card to your computer, the old pictures are deleted from the card. However, this doesn't delete protected images or fix issues with the card. It's better to format the card each time you want it empty, except when you want to keep some protected images for a bit longer to share.

- **(Don't) Format in your computer:** Insert the memory card into your computer's card reader. Avoid reformatting it using Windows or Mac OS since they might set it up in a way your camera doesn't like. Always format the card directly in the camera to ensure the right Format for your camera. The only exception is when the card is severely corrupted, in which case you might try letting the operating system reformat it first before attempting a camera format.

- **Set-up menu format:** To properly format a memory card using the suggested method, follow these steps:

  1. Press MENU.

  2. Keep pressing INFO until you see a wrench icon.

  3. Turn the big dial to choose Set-up 1.

  4. Use the small dial on top to select Format Card in Set-up 1.

  5. Press SET to confirm.

  6. Turn the small dial to highlight OK, then press SET to start the Format. You can also press INFO before to do a thorough format if the card has been used often.

CHAPTER 2: FOCUS

Exploring Viewfinder Focusing Options

Focus Mode

In photography, Focus Mode refers to the setting that controls how your camera focuses on a subject. It essentially dictates whether the camera will automatically focus for you (autofocus) or if you'll be focusing manually.

Here's how you can pick how the Canon EOS R50 focuses:

1. Select Focus mode.

2. Choose between AF (Auto Focus) and MF (Manual Focus).

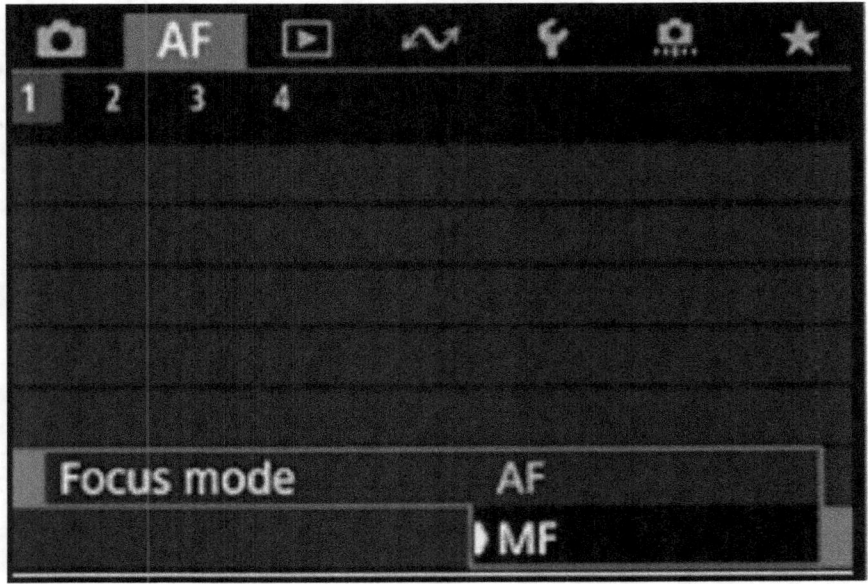

23

Manually Setting AF Points or Zone Frames

You can choose where the camera focuses by manually setting the Zone AF frame or AF point. If you pick Flexible Zone AF 1, follow these steps:

1. See where the camera is focusing (AF point).

2. Move the focus to a different point if needed. Use the buttons to move the AF point, but note that it might not reach the screen's edge with some lenses.

3. Pay attention and either record or take a shot.

Magnified View

Tap the magnifying option to make the display 5 or 10 times bigger and check the focus. To zoom in on the image, press the button and then the <INFO> button.

When the box around the person is white, the camera zooms in on them. If the box is gray or there's no person detected, it zooms in on the center. If you press the shutter button halfway, it zooms in even more for focusing. In Servo AF or AI Focus AF modes, pressing halfway switches back to the normal view for focusing.

AF Shooting Tips

Photography enthusiasts may encounter difficulties in achieving precise focus, particularly when faced with changes in ambient light or screen flickering during the image capture process. When such challenges arise, a recommended course of action is to restart the camera and utilize the autofocus (AF) function under the preferred light source.

In certain situations, the autofocus feature may struggle to perform optimally. If this is the case, manually adjusting the focus becomes a viable alternative. This involves centering the subject or aligning the autofocus point with the desired focal point. By doing so, photographers can bring elements into clear focus, particularly if there is blurriness at the edges of the frame.

It's essential to note that different lenses may exhibit variations in autofocus performance. Some lenses may take longer to achieve focus, while others may face difficulties in focusing accurately through the autofocus mechanism. In such instances, employing manual focus provides greater control over the focusing process, allowing photographers to fine-tune the focus point according to their preferences.

Shooting conditions that make focusing difficult

- Objects like the blue sky, flat things of one color, and when there are too bright or dark areas.

- Things in low light.

- Patterns that mostly go side to side, like stripes.

- Things with repeated designs, like computer keyboards and tall building windows.

- Shapes and thin lines.

- In places where the light changes a lot at night.

- The picture might flicker under certain lights like fluorescent or LED, especially with very small or edge-of-screen subjects.

- Like shiny cars, subjects with strong backlighting or reflections can be tricky. The autofocus (AF) point might cover close and far objects, like a caged animal, and subjects that move a lot due to camera shake or blur.

- AF is used when the subject is very blurry, and a soft focus lens or special filter might be used for a soft focus effect.

- Remember that you might see screen noise like light dots or banding during AF.

Manual Focus

Manual focus is a camera setting that allows you, the photographer, to take control of the focusing process instead of relying on the camera's autofocus system. This means you physically adjust the lens's focus ring until your subject appears sharp and clear in the viewfinder or on the camera's screen.

If the camera can't focus automatically, make the picture bigger and focus yourself. Here's how you can use the Manual Focus:

1. Choose the <MF> focus mode.

2. Zoom in on the image.

3. Move the zoomed-in part.

   - Use arrow keys to adjust the position.

   - Press <MENU> to center the zoomed area.

4. Focus manually.

   - Turn the lens' focus ring to sharpen the magnified image.

   - Press a button to go back to the normal view once focused.

Setting MF Peaking (Outline Emphasis)

Setting MF Peaking, also known as Outline Emphasis, is a visual aid for manual focus in cameras. It highlights in-focus areas of your subject with a colored outline, making it easier to achieve precise sharpness, especially when using lenses with a shallow depth of field.

To help you focus better, you can see color-coded edges around things that are in focus. Just follow these steps:

1. Go to MF Peaking Settings.

2. Turn on "Peaking."

3. Pick a color and adjust the level.

AF Area

Canon's AF area is like a tool that decides which parts of the camera's view are used for focusing. You can choose from eight AF area modes to pick where the focus starts or which zone it covers. You can also turn on or off subject tracking, allowing the camera to follow and focus on people, animals, or vehicles. I'll talk more about subject tracking later.

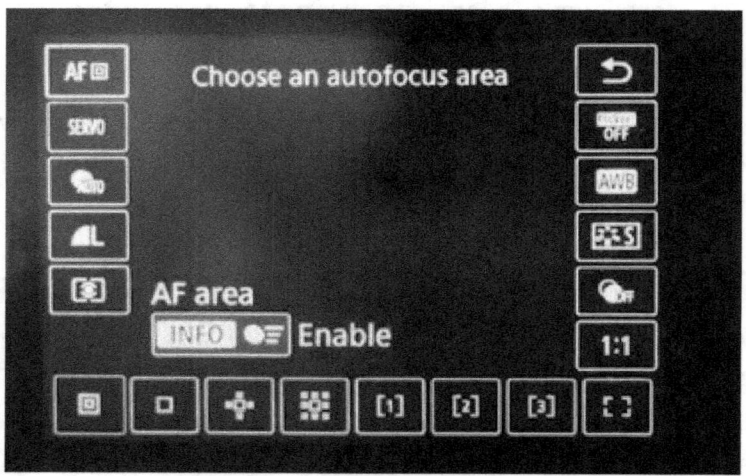

Switching between autofocus modes is simple: press the AF selection button on the upper-right corner of the camera's back panel, then press the M-Fn button repeatedly to cycle through available modes displayed on the screen. While choosing an autofocus method, you can use the INFO button to turn subject tracking on/off. If you prefer using only a few autofocus modes, you can hide the others by accessing the Limit AF Methods entry in the AF 4 menu under AF Area.

I'll talk about each of the eight AF methods one by one. A specific AF method, like Spot AF, stays the same whether you're taking pictures horizontally or vertically. But later, I'll explain that you can choose different AF methods and focus points for each orientation, which can be helpful for specific subjects.

Spot AF

In this mode, you can zoom in and concentrate on a small box on the screen. You can move this focus area little by little to almost any spot on the screen using the Multi-controller joystick or the Main Dial (for left/right movement) or QCD (for up/down movement). Press the AF point selection button first to start moving the focus point.

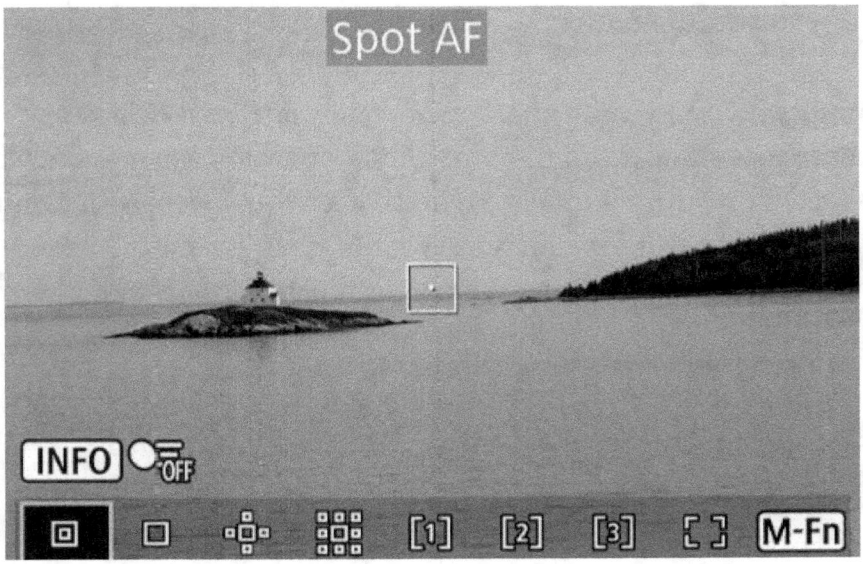

Using this precision setting on your camera is excellent but can have drawbacks. When the camera or subject moves, the focus might shift away from your main subject. This mode is useful when you need to focus very precisely on a subject with lots of fine details around it. It's handy for scenes where you want to focus on a specific point, especially if your subject moves slowly.

Adjust the focus point using the controls. Use this mode for everyday shooting when you need precision and the subject has enough detail in the sensor's area. If a small part of your subject is unclear, you can use other focus modes described later, considering surrounding focus points and the one you manually select.

1-Point AF

In this mode, you can zoom in and concentrate on a box about three times bigger on the screen. It's great for when you need speed but still want to pinpoint where to focus with some accuracy. I use it for sports, especially when I want to highlight specific players who aren't moving much, like an infielder at third base. You can easily adjust the focus point.

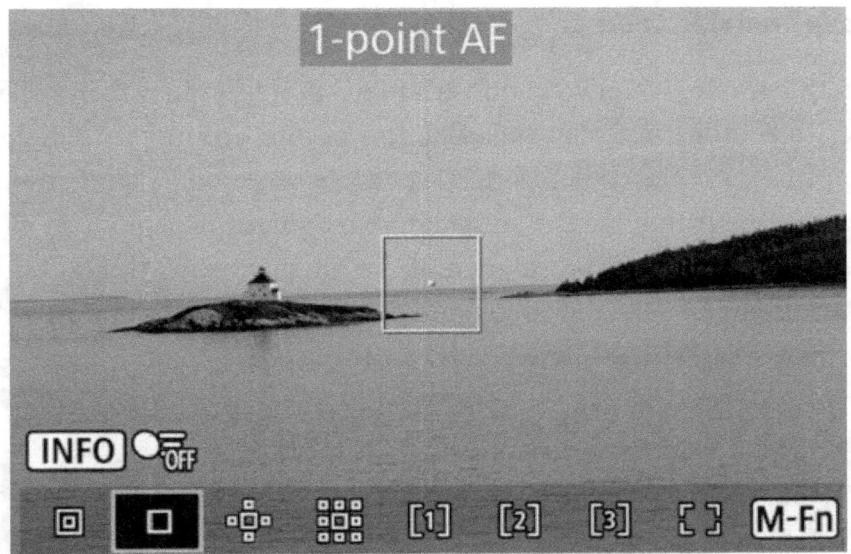

How it works:

1. Navigate your camera's menu to find the AF area setting and choose "1-point AF."

2. Use the multi-selector buttons or touchscreen to move the single AF point around the frame. You can even drag it to adjust its size for larger or smaller subjects.

3. Once the point is positioned over your desired focus area, press the shutter button halfway down. The camera will focus on that specific spot, indicated by a green or blue square around the point (green for One-Shot AF and blue for Servo AF).

Expand AF Area

In this mode, when you choose a focus point, it not only focuses on that point but also includes the points around it. It helps capture moving objects since the larger zone helps track them within the frame. As the subject moves, surrounding points can continue tracking its movement. In One-Shot AF mode, both the manually selected focus point and the expanded point will be shown.

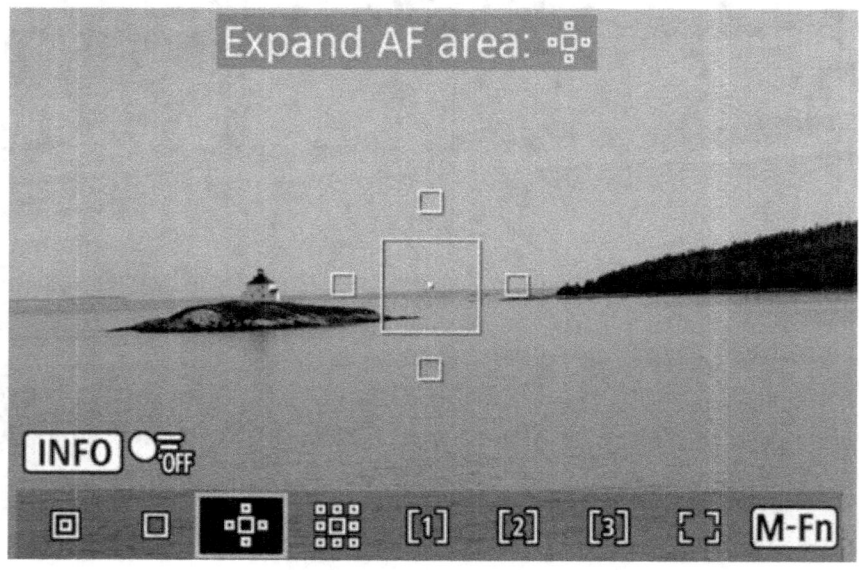

This is particularly helpful when:

- **Your subject is small or fast-moving:** Having extra AF points surrounding your target increases the chance of capturing accurate focus, even if the subject moves slightly.

- **You're anticipating movement:** If your subject is about to shift, Expand AF Area gives the camera a buffer zone to maintain focus as they move.

- **Precise manual focusing is challenging:** By expanding the focus area, you can easily achieve sharp focus using manual focus peaking or magnification, especially on textured subjects.

Here's how to use expand AF area:

1. Navigate to the AF area settings in your camera's menu and choose either "Expand AF area: Around" or "Expand AF area: Above/Below/Left/Right."

2. Use the multi-selector buttons or touchscreen to move the single AF point to your desired focus area.

3. Press the shutter button halfway down. The camera will focus on the selected point and activate the surrounding expanded AF points for added accuracy.

Expand AF Area: Around

This mode is like the one above, but it includes the eight nearby points when you choose a point to focus on. It works well for things without much detail at the chosen focus point; the extra points around it improve your results. It's also good for bigger moving objects, even though it's less precise. Remember, you can move the active area around on the display while seeing the points in the center.

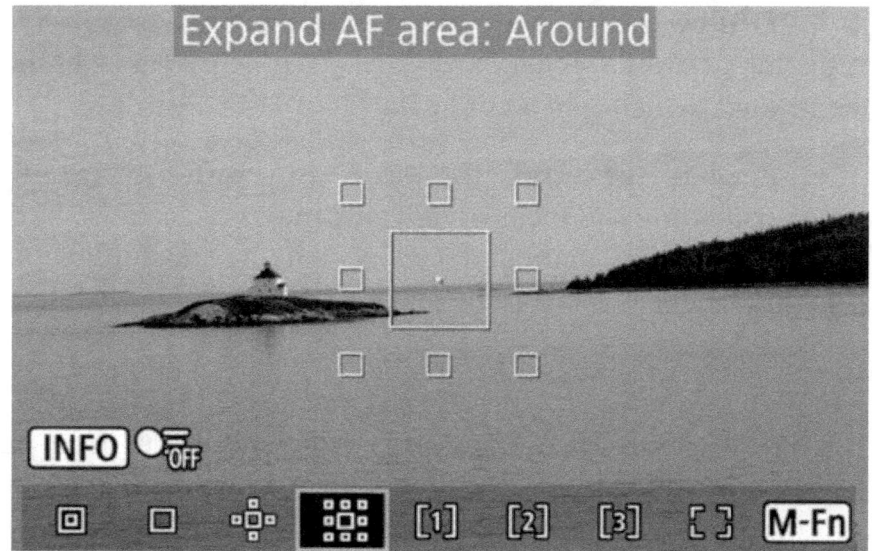

Flexible Zone AF 1

This method divides your focus points into a zone, like a square on your camera screen. When you adjust the focus, you move this zone around the frame. It's useful when you roughly know where your subject is and want to focus on that area. However, it may not be as precise as other focus methods. To shift the zone, press the AF point selection button and use the directional buttons or other controls mentioned earlier.

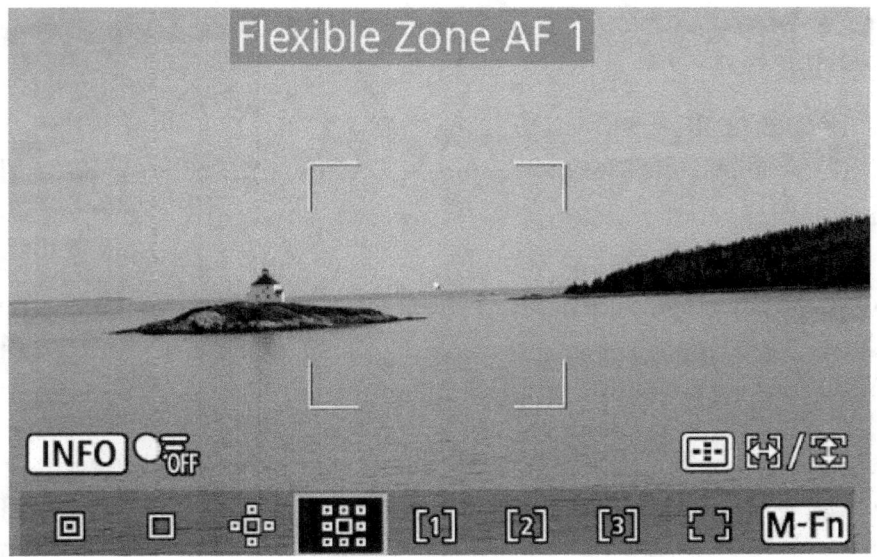

Unlike Flexible Zone AF 2 and 3, which offer predefined rectangular shapes, Zone AF 1 grants you complete freedom to draw and resize your own autofocus zone directly on the touchscreen or using the multi-selector buttons. This means you can:

- **Create any shape:** Design triangles, circles, or even freehand squiggles to precisely match your subject's form or compositional intent.

- **Focus on small, intricate details:** Encircle a tiny bird's eye or a flower's stamen for pinpoint focus accuracy.

- **Track unique movements:** Follow an erratic butterfly's flight or a child's unpredictable dance with a custom-shaped zone.

Flexible Zone AF 2 (Vertical)/Flexible Zone AF 3 (Horizontal)

The Canon EOS R50's Dual Pixel CMOS AF II system offers a unique feature: Flexible Zone AF. This mode goes beyond predefined focus areas, allowing you to customize the size and shape of the autofocus zone for precise control over where the camera focuses. Let's explore the two specific options – Flexible Zone AF 2 (Vertical) and Flexible Zone AF 3 (Horizontal) – and how they can enhance your photography:

These two methods use big rectangular areas that can be tall or wide, depending on what you need. One is suitable for tall things like basketball, and the other for wide scenes like motorsports or boat racing. The camera will automatically pick the right focus points, usually on the closest subject, and look for faces to focus on.

Flexible Zone AF 2 (Vertical)

Imagine a rectangle standing tall within your viewfinder. This is Flexible Zone AF 2.

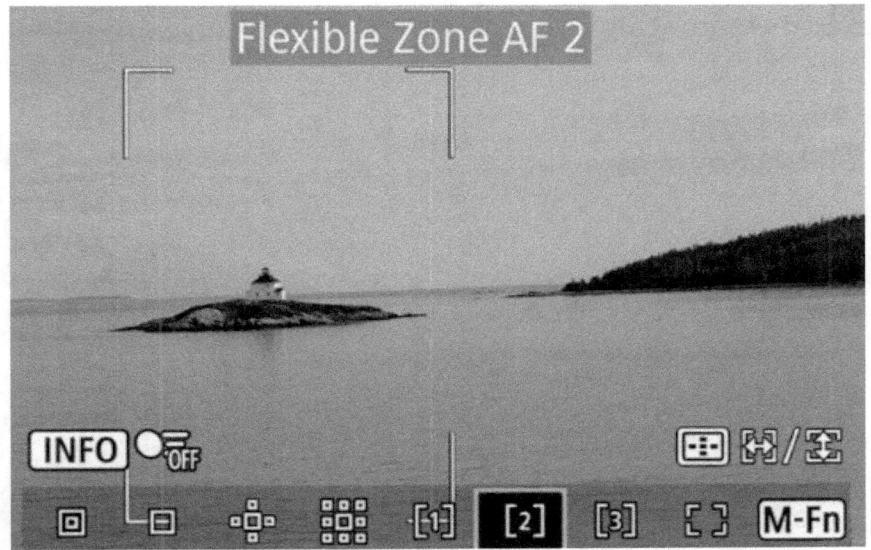

By default, it's a narrower zone, ideal for situations like:

- **Portraiture:** Precisely focus on your subject's eyes, even if they're slightly off-center.

- **Macro photography:** Achieve sharp focus on intricate details of flowers or insects.

- **Following moving subjects:** Track subjects vertically, like a bird in flight or a dancer leaping.

Flexible Zone AF 3 (Horizontal):

Think of a rectangle lying down on your viewfinder — that's Flexible Zone AF 3.

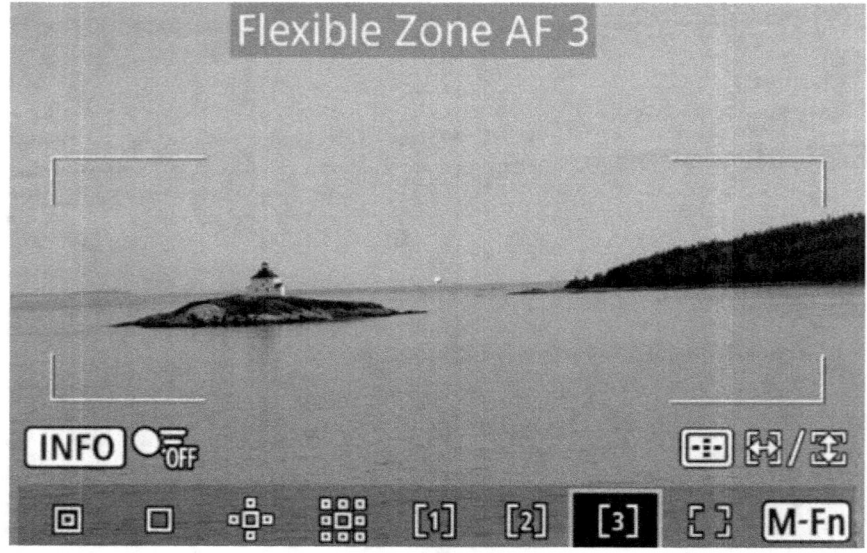

This wider zone is perfect for:

- **Landscape photography:** Focus on a specific element in the foreground while keeping the background sharp.

- **Capturing wide movements:** Track subjects moving horizontally, like cars racing or athletes sprinting.

- **Group shots:** Ensure everyone's eyes are in focus, especially when they're lined up horizontally.

Whole Area AF

In this mode, the R50 automatically picks where to focus on the picture. It works well for fast-moving things, like in sports, where picking a focus area yourself is hard. When this mode and Subject Tracking are on, you can quickly tap the screen to choose a face or eye.

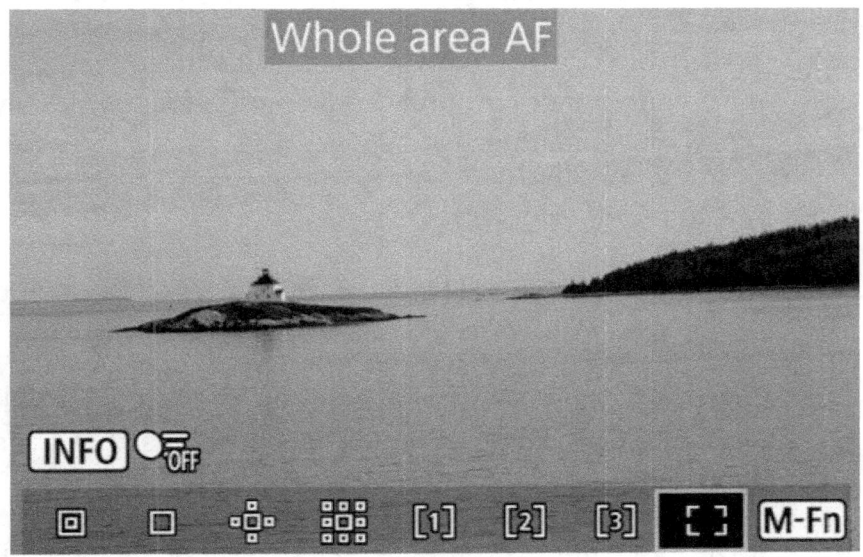

Unlike other AF modes that limit the focusing area, Whole Area AF utilizes all 651 of the camera's AF points across the entire frame. This means the camera continuously tracks and focuses on your subject, no matter where it moves within the viewfinder.

Think of it as a focus net covering your entire frame, constantly seeking and maintaining sharp focus on your chosen subject. It's ideal for:

- **Fast-paced action:** Capture crisp shots of sports, wildlife, or children at play without worrying about losing focus as they move.

39

- **Unpredictable movement:** Shooting birds in flight, dancers on stage, or street performers becomes effortless as the camera tracks their every movement.

- **Dynamic compositions:** Shoot with the freedom to move your camera around, knowing the focus will stay locked on your subject.

Here's how to use Whole Area AF:

1. Navigate to the AF area settings in your camera's menu and choose "Whole Area AF."

2. Half-press the shutter button and the camera will automatically select a focusing point based on its algorithms and track it across the frame.

3. Move your camera around, reframe the shot, or zoom in, and the camera will maintain focus on your subject.

CHAPTER 3: MASTERING COLOR CONTROLS

Understanding the White Balance Setting

White things look white in different lights because our eyes adjust. Cameras use image processing to make colors look real by determining what's white based on the lighting's color temperature.

Adjusting the White Balance setting

White balance helps make white areas appear truly white in a photo. You can achieve the correct white balance by choosing Ambience or White priority. If the Auto mode doesn't show realistic colors, you can manually adjust the white balance by photographing something white or selecting a balance that matches the light source.

1. Pick White balance.

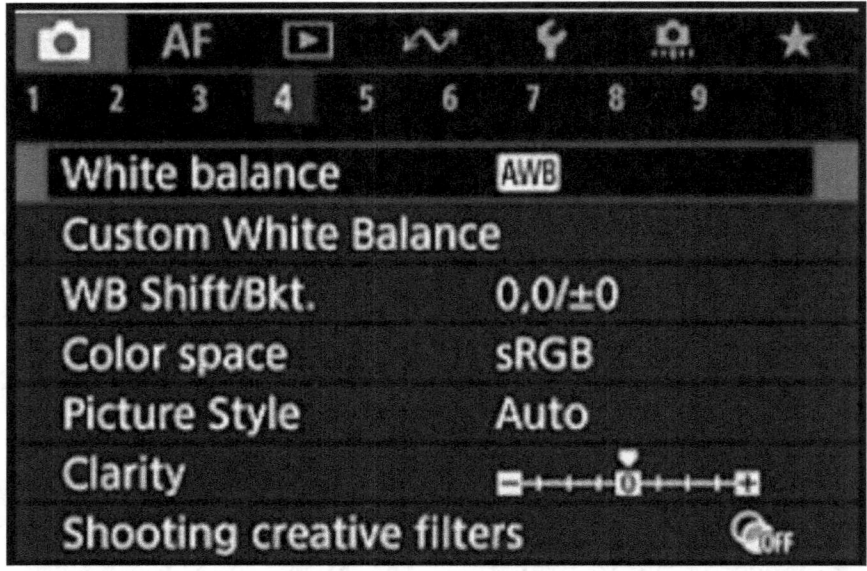

2. Select an option.

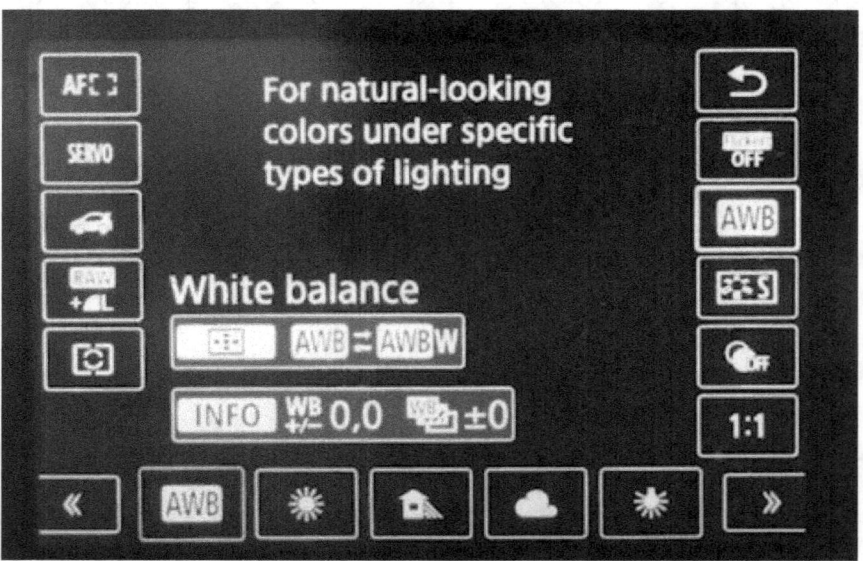

To adjust the white balance, turn the mode dial left or right.

Auto White Balance

The Canon EOS R50's Auto White Balance (AWB) mode takes the guesswork out of achieving natural-looking colors in your photos. It's a great starting point for beginners and a convenient option for everyday shooting, but understanding its strengths and limitations can help you get the most out of it.

To make a photo with warmer colors in a tungsten-light setting:

1. Pick White Balance.

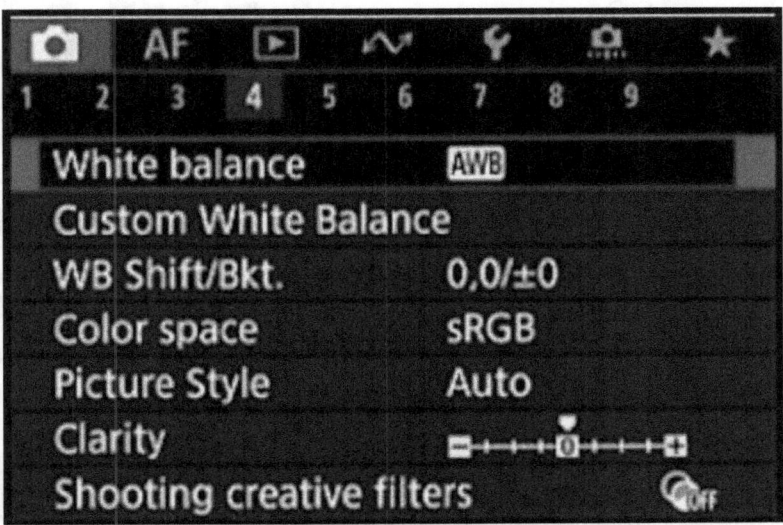

2. Click on [AWB].

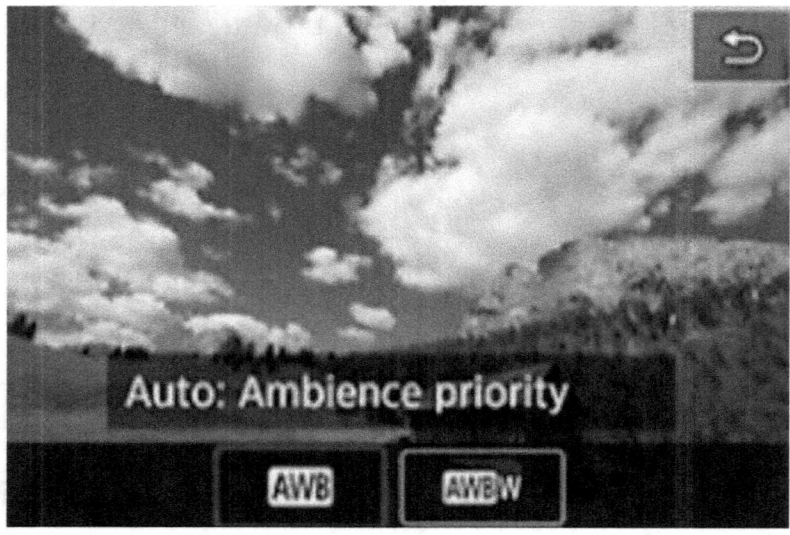

3. Press the + button while [AWB] is selected, then choose an option.

Creating a custom White Balance setting

Setting the white balance manually is a fundamental aspect of achieving color accuracy in your photographs. White balance refers to the color temperature of the light sources illuminating your scene. When the white balance is correctly adjusted, it ensures that whites appear neutral, and colors are rendered faithfully, reflecting the true tones present in the scene.

To set the white balance manually, it's advisable to do so on-site, where the actual lighting conditions prevail. This involves assessing the ambient light and adjusting the camera settings accordingly. Modern digital cameras offer a range of white balance presets, such as daylight, cloudy, shade, tungsten, and fluorescent, among others. However, these presets might not always perfectly match the unique lighting conditions of your specific environment.

By setting the white balance manually on-site, you take into account the nuanced color temperature of the light present in the scene. This can be done by using a neutral reference, such as a white or gray card. Some photographers prefer to use a custom white balance setting, which involves capturing an image of the neutral reference under the prevailing lighting conditions and instructing the camera to use that image as the reference for accurate color reproduction.

Doing this on-site is crucial because lighting conditions can vary widely from one location to another, even within the same day. The color temperature of natural light changes throughout the day, and artificial lighting sources introduce their unique color casts. Manually adjusting the white balance on-site allows you to account for these variations, resulting in more accurate and true-to-life colors in your photographs.

Registration from an Image on a card

1. Take a picture of something white.

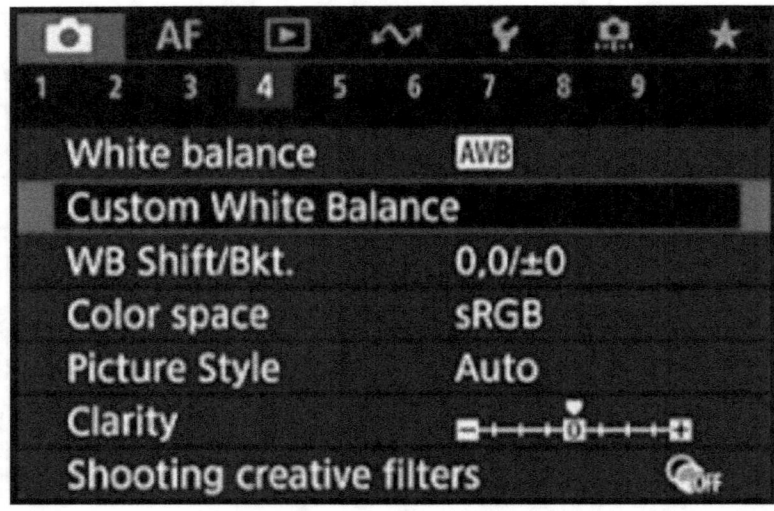

2. Pick Custom White Balance next.

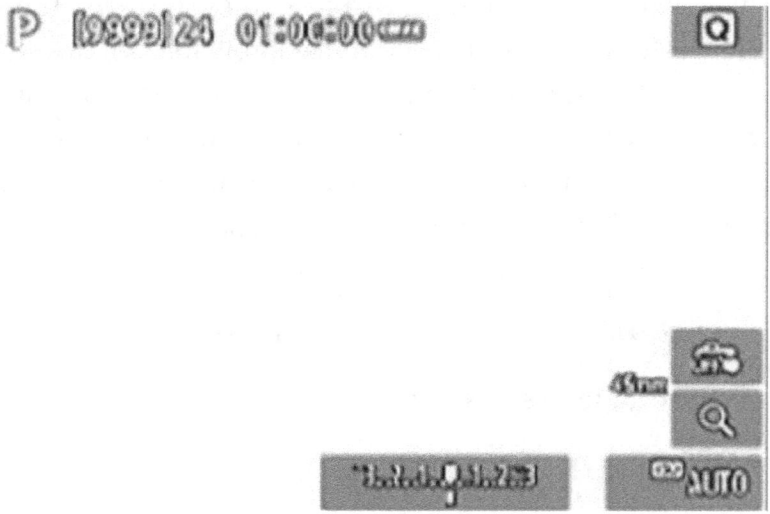

3. Use the arrow keys to select the white object photo from step 1. Click [OK] to bring in the data.

4. Opt for [: White balance].

5. Select the option shown in the image.

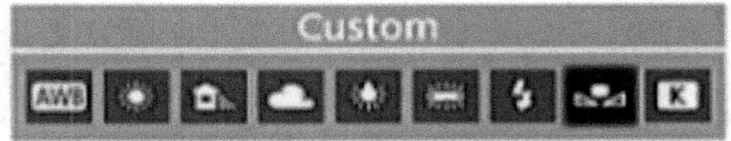

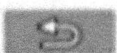

Shooting and registering white balance

1. Start by pressing the SET button.

2. Select a white balance setting.

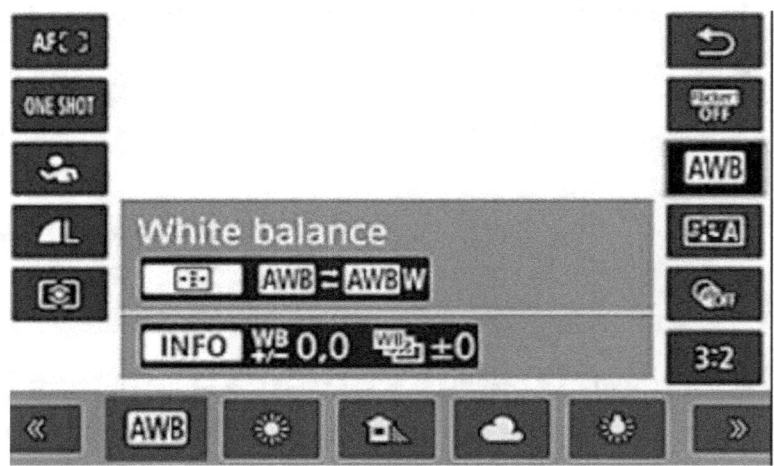

3. Opt for "Shoot to set WB."

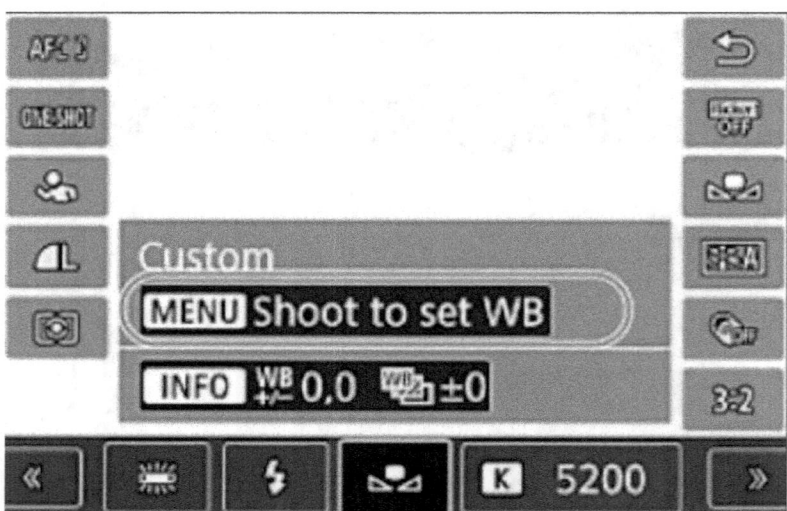

4. Take a picture of a white object.

Color Temperature

The Canon EOS R50 presents you with a fascinating tool beyond automatic settings: Color Temperature. Understanding this concept and its practical application will broaden your creative range and empower you to manipulate the mood and atmosphere of your photographs.

Think of color temperature like the "warmth" or "coolness" of light, measured in degrees Kelvin (K). Sunlight at midday holds a high color temperature (around 5500K), appearing cool and crisp. Tungsten lamps, on the other hand, emit light with a low color temperature (around 3200K), lending a warm, yellowish glow.

The color temperature of the light source influences how colors are captured by your camera. A shot under warm incandescent light might appear overly yellow, while cool daylight can make whites seem bluish. This is where color temperature control comes in.

Your EOS R50 offers various options to manipulate color temperature:

- **Auto White Balance (AWB):** This automatically analyzes the light and adjusts the color balance to achieve neutral whites. Ideal for everyday shooting, but less precise in complex lighting.

- **Preset White Balance:** Choose from predefined settings like Daylight, Shade, Tungsten, etc., to match the dominant light source for more accurate color rendition.

- **Custom White Balance:** Capture a neutral reference using a white card under the specific lighting conditions, providing the most precise white balance for that scene.

- **Kelvin White Balance:** Manually set the desired color temperature in degrees Kelvin for complete control, from warm candlelight to cool moonlight.

To adjust the color of your photos, follow these steps:

1. Pick White Balance.

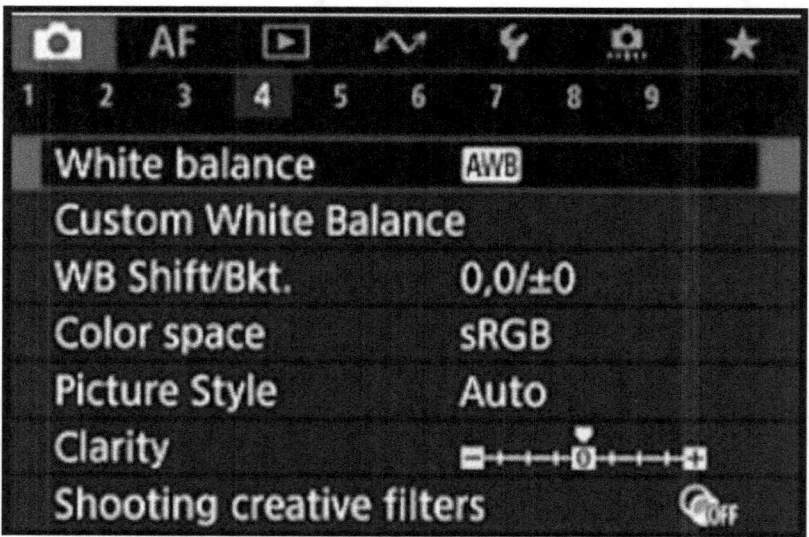

2. Choose a color temperature by pressing the + button with [K] selected.

Set the color temperature by turning the mode dial and pressing SET.

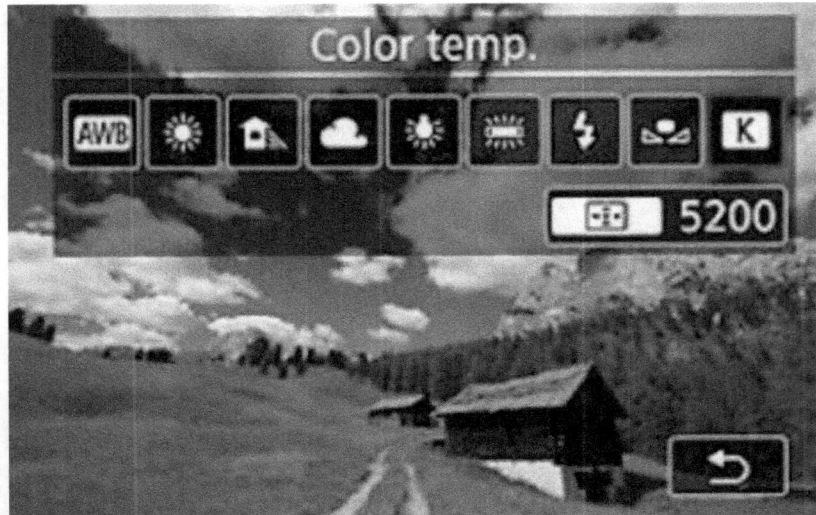

3. You can tweak the color temperature in 100K steps between 2500K and 10000K.

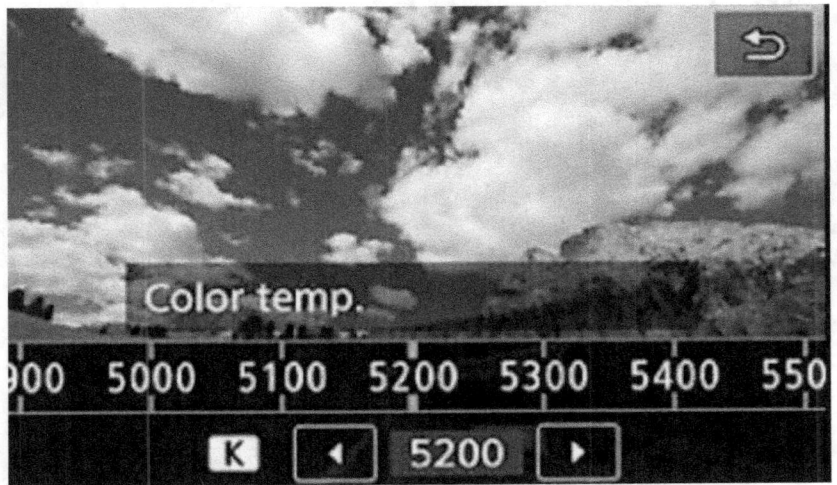

White balance correction

While Auto White Balance (AWB) on your Canon EOS R50 strives to achieve natural colors in most situations, sometimes it might not hit the mark perfectly. That's where White Balance Correction comes in, offering you the power to fine-tune the color balance and achieve precise, impactful results in your photos.

Here's how to use the white balance correction:

1. Start by choosing WB Shift/Bkt.

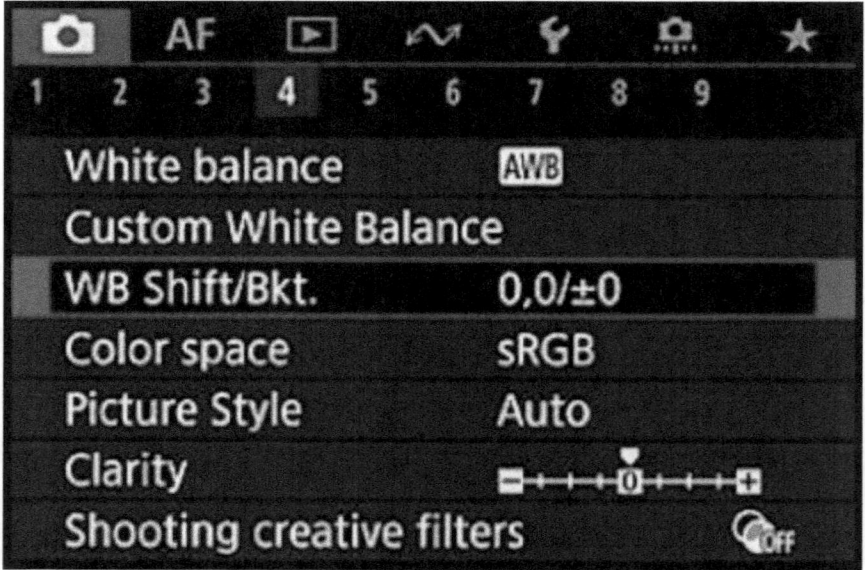

2. Change the white balance by moving the box on the screen using the arrow keys.

- A is for amber, M is for magenta, and G is for green.

- The white balance shifts as you move the box.

- In the top right, you'll see arrows showing the correction direction and strength.

- Press the button to cancel any WB Shift/Bkt. Changes.

- Finish the setup by pressing the button.

White Balance Bracketing

When you use WB bracketing on your camera, it takes one photo and creates several different versions with varying color balances. You can adjust the blue/amber or magenta/green bias using the Main Dial or QCD. After setting the bias, use the Multi-controller joystick to fine-tune the color balance. Most of the time, you won't need detailed adjustments – making images bluer/yellower or more green/magenta is usually enough.

The only times you might need clarification about color temperatures are when warmer colors (more reddish) have lower numbers and cooler colors (bluer) have higher numbers. So, 3,400K is warmer than 6,000K, which seems odd, but you can think of mparing a red ember to a white-hot welder's torch instead of fire and ice.

Scientists get confused because they use a theoretical thing called a black body radiator in physics to calculate color temperature. This imaginary object absorbs all incoming energy and reflects none, making it perfect in theory, but since perfection doesn't exist, it's considered mythical.

This made-up thing always gives off light of the same color at a specific temperature. We measure this color temperature in degrees Kelvin, like how scientists do. For instance, regular light bulbs are around 3,200K to 3,400K, while daylight is between 5,500K and 6,000K. Different lights in photography have their color temperatures, but be careful about that.

Taking a Quick Look at Picture Styles

How to Select a Picture Style

Select a preset Picture Style to match the emotions or theme of your photos. Just follow these steps:

1. Pick a Picture Style.

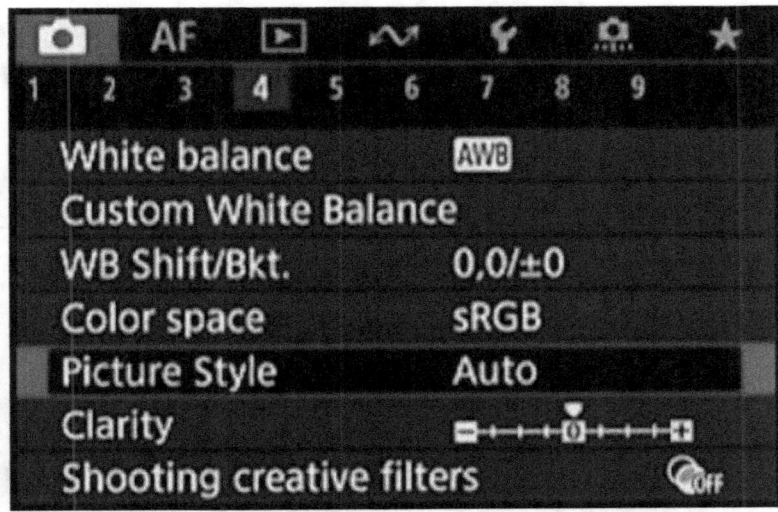

2. Choose the one you like.

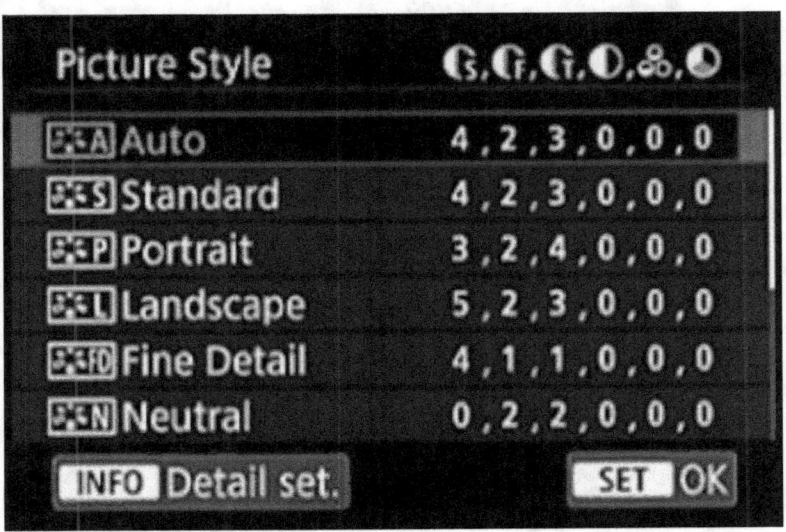

Picture Style Characteristics

Auto

The colors will adjust automatically to match the surroundings. In nature pictures, like outdoors or sunsets, the colors will look vivid against the blue sky, lush plants, and sunsets.

Standard

The images look sharp, vivid, and lively in most scenes.

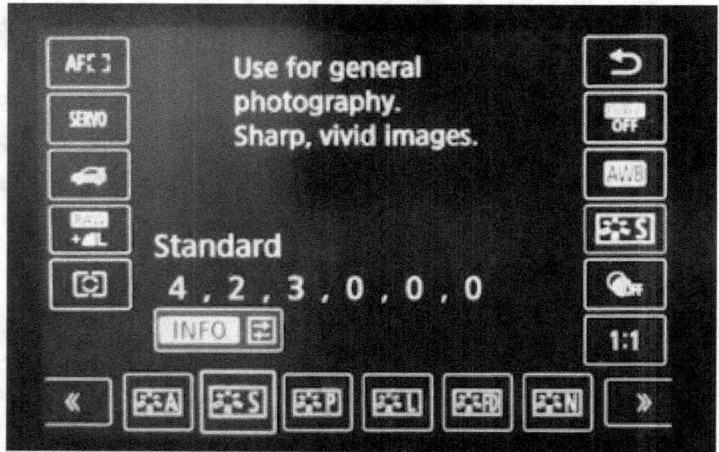

Portrait

Make skin look smoother and more natural in close-up photos by adjusting the [Color tone] settings in Settings and Effects.

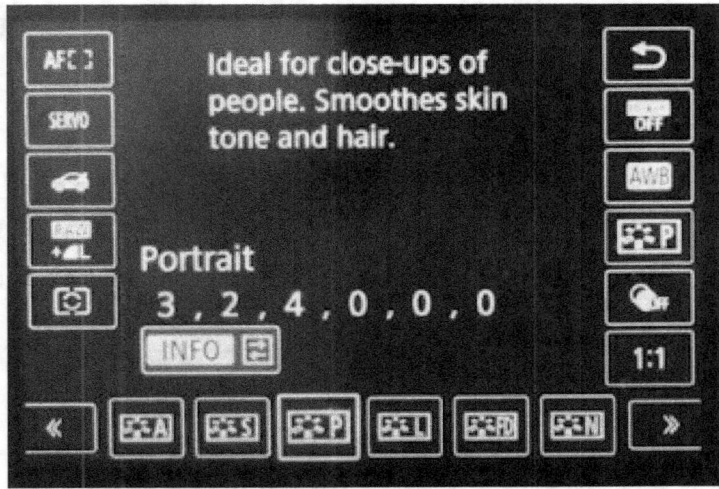

Landscape

Capture vivid and sharp photos with vibrant blue and green colors, perfect for capturing breathtaking landscapes.

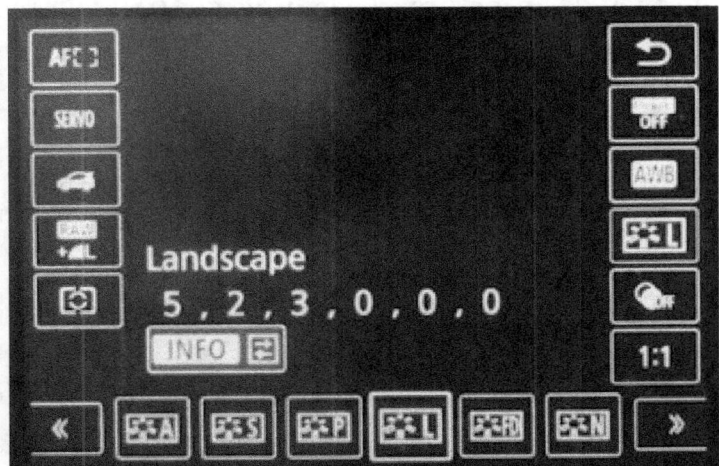

Fine Details

Show gentle details and subtle textures with vibrant colors.

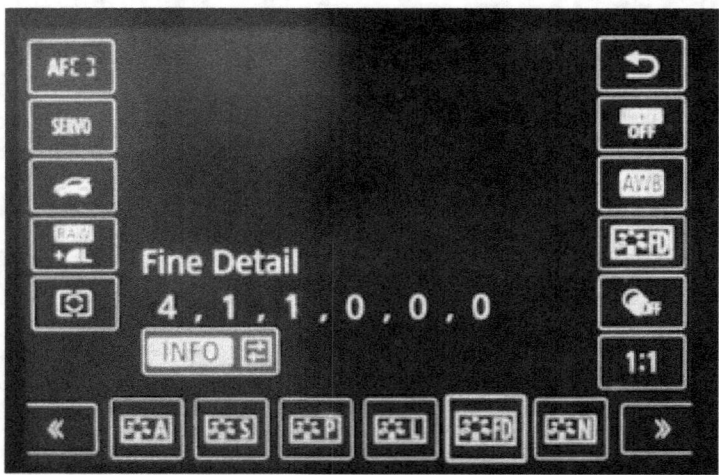

Faithful

It is suitable for editing photos on a computer. It makes colors look like they do in natural daylight at 5200K. The result is softer, less contrasting pictures.

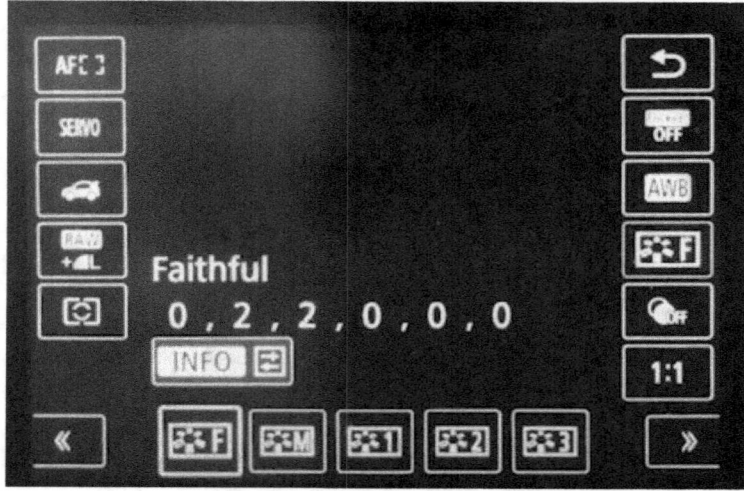

Monochrome

Black and white pictures are created when using monochrome settings.

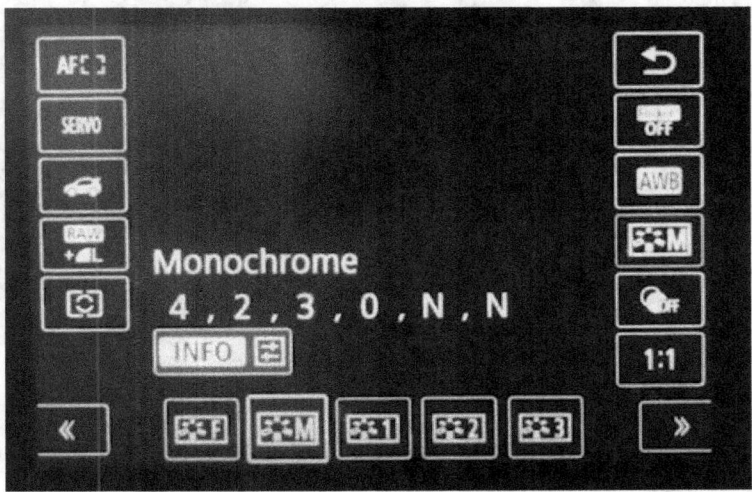

User Def. 1-3

You can add a picture style or create a new one from presets like [Portrait] or [Landscape]. Customize it as needed. Pictures will be like the default [Auto] preset if you don't pick a style.

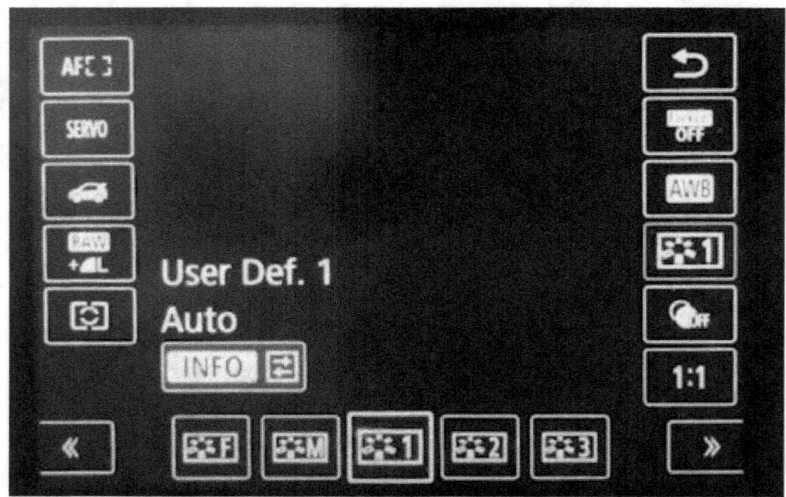

Picture Style Customization

You can change how a Picture Style looks by adjusting its original settings.

1. Select a Picture Style.

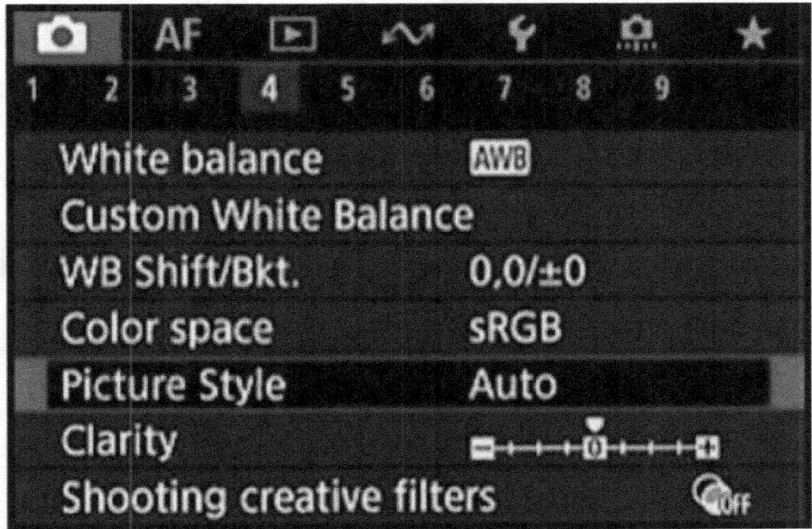

2. Pick the style you want.

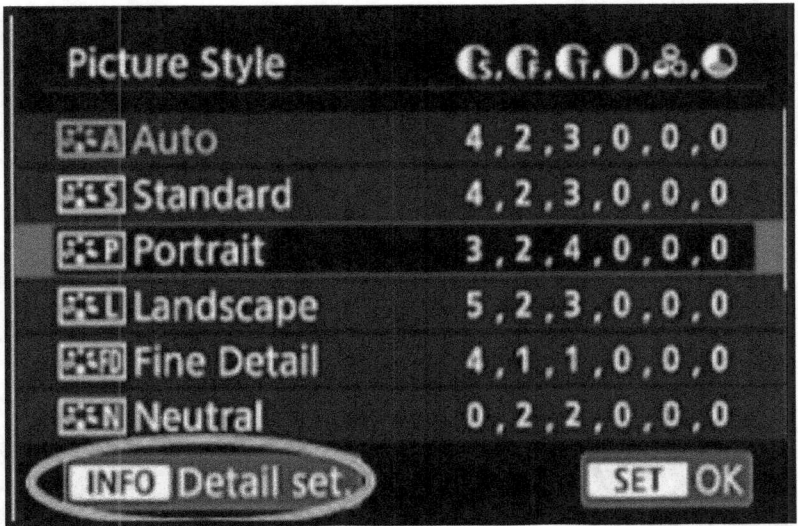

Click INFO after choosing.

3. Choose an option.

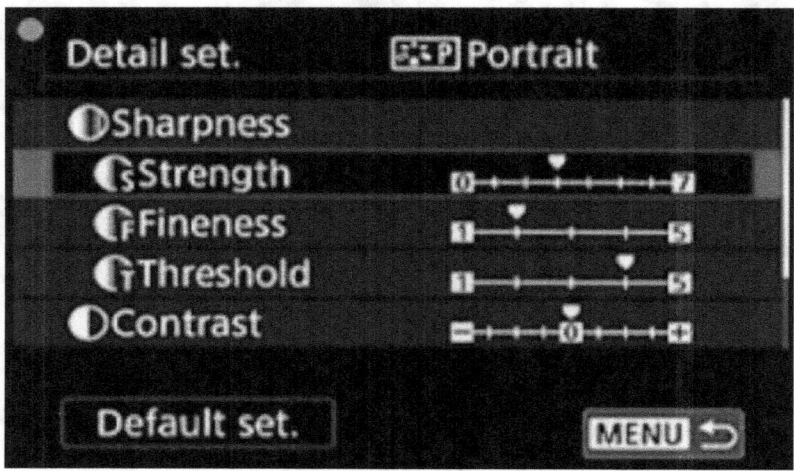

Press SET after choosing.

4. Adjust the effect level.

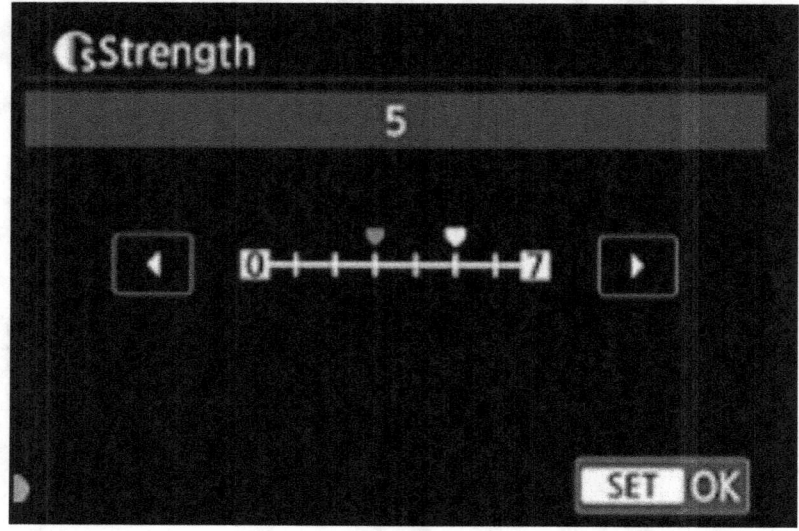

Press SET after adjusting.

Save by using the MENU button.

Altered settings are shown in blue.

Picture Style Registration

1. Pick a Picture Style.

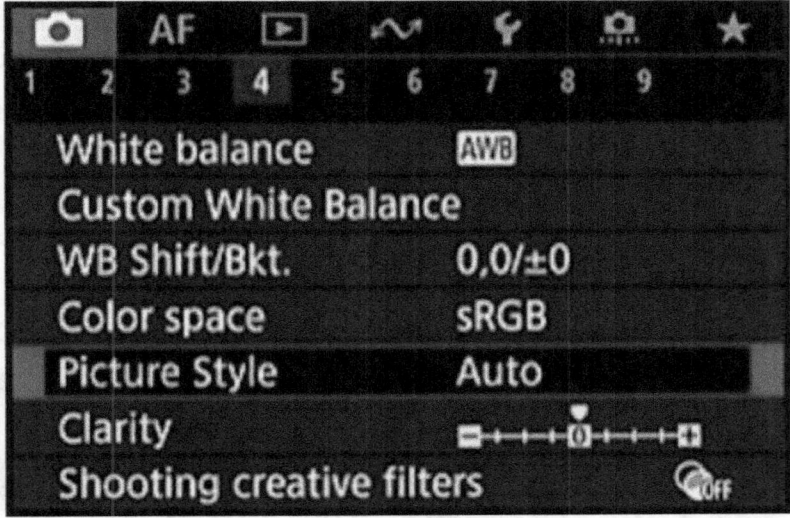

2. Choose [User Def].

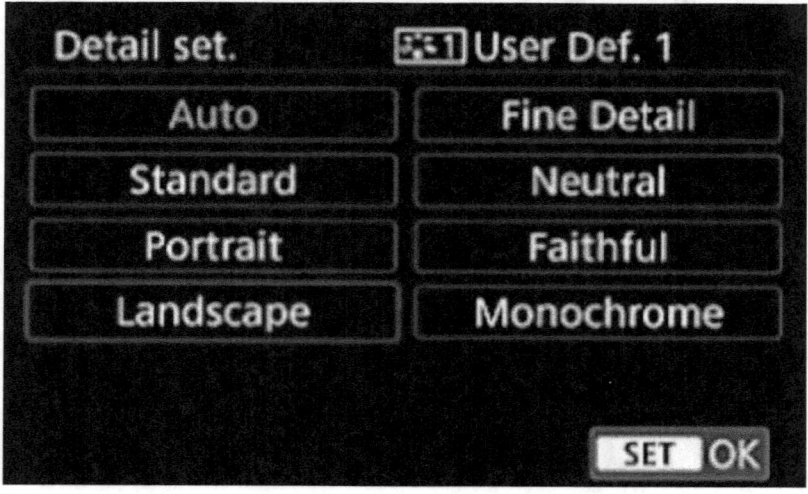

Click INFO after selecting [User Def. *].

3. Select [Picture Style] and click SET.

4. Choose a base Picture Style and press SET.

If modifying styles with EOS Utility, pick styles similarly.

5. Choose an option and press the button.

6. Pick the effect level and press the button.

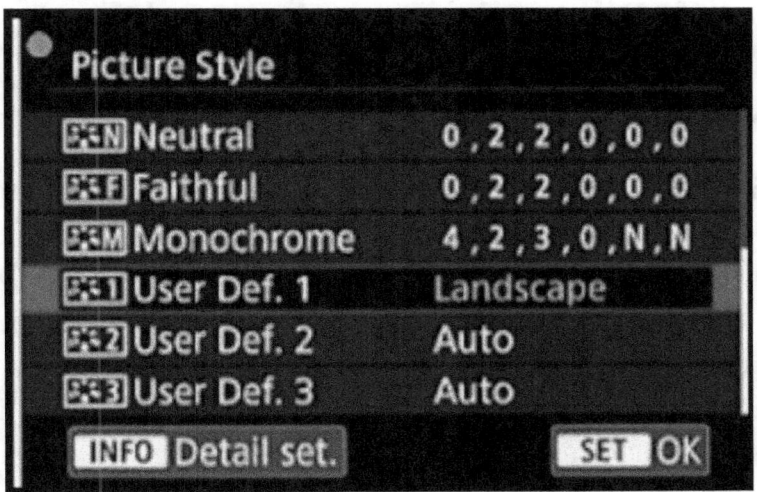

CHAPTER 4: CHOOSING BASIC PICTURE SETTINGS

Discovering Basic Zone Modes

Scene Intelligent Auto Mode

At first glance, having a mode on the advanced R50 camera with few user options may seem strange, turning it into a simple point-and-shoot camera. However, if you explore further, you'll find that Canon's Scene Intelligent Auto goes beyond just a basic mode and has some clever features, making it more than a limited Program mode. The crucial aspect is the intelligent part of the mode's name.

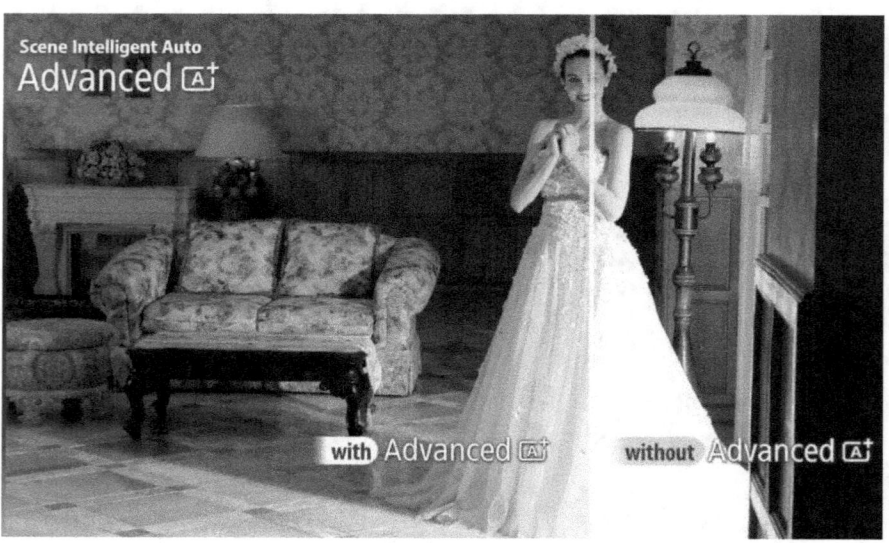

The camera sets shutter speed and aperture in P mode, but you can adjust other things. In Scene Intelligent Auto mode, the camera analyzes your scene, considers if your subject is still or moving, and picks the best settings without you doing anything.

The camera can be adjusted using these settings:

- **ISO speed:** The camera will pick the ISO level by itself.

- **Picture Style:** The camera is set to Automatic Picture Style, which will pick the right settings. If you adjusted Auto Picture Style, those changes won't apply in Scene Intelligent Auto mode.

- **White balance:** The camera adjusts colors by itself, and you can't manually change it.

- **Auto Lighting Optimizer:** Always in the smart auto mode for scenes.

- **Color space:** Changed to sRGB without a choice.

- **Autofocus:** When you press the halfway button on the camera, it automatically chooses between One-Shot AF and Servo AF. You can't manually switch between them. The camera also independently picks the autofocus (AF) point, and the AF-assist beam helps if necessary. To toggle Eye Detection, press the Q/SET button, select the AF Method icon, and press the INFO button.

- **Metering mode:** Evaluative metering is always in use.

When you turn the Mode Dial to A+, a screen pops up. Press OK, and the view on the right appears on the touch screen. Look for an icon in the upper-left corner showing the camera's chosen scene mode (like Portrait). On the left side are icons for the three settings you can adjust using the touch screen.

- **Image quality/size:** Touch the icon to choose between RAW, JPEG, and different image sizes, including Movie Recording Size.

- **Drive mode:** Tap the icon between taking one picture, three pictures in a row at different speeds, or using a self-timer with 2 or 10-second delays. There's also a mode where the camera continuously takes 2 to 10 shots after the timer runs out.

- **Touch Shutter (Enable/Disable):** If you turn on Touch Shutter, tap on someone's face or anything in the picture, and it will take a photo.

- **Manual focus:** You can pick manual focus by switching the AF/MF button on the camera's front or the lens (if it has one), along with the three mentioned settings.

- **Creative Assist:** In the bottom-right corner of the screen, you'll find the lens zoom setting and a button for Creative Assist, which I'll explain later. The camera has a smart mode called Scene Intelligent. It guesses the type of scene you're capturing and applies the appropriate settings automatically. The chosen scene is shown as an icon in the top-left corner of the screen.

Creative Assist

Scene Intelligent Auto's Creative Assist is a tool for making your photos look excellent. If you're using A+, just tap the Creative Assist icon on the screen or press the Q/SET button. Then, you'll see a list of effects you can use, like Background Blur, Brightness, Contrast, and more. Pick the one you want, adjust it using the sliders, and make your photos stand out!

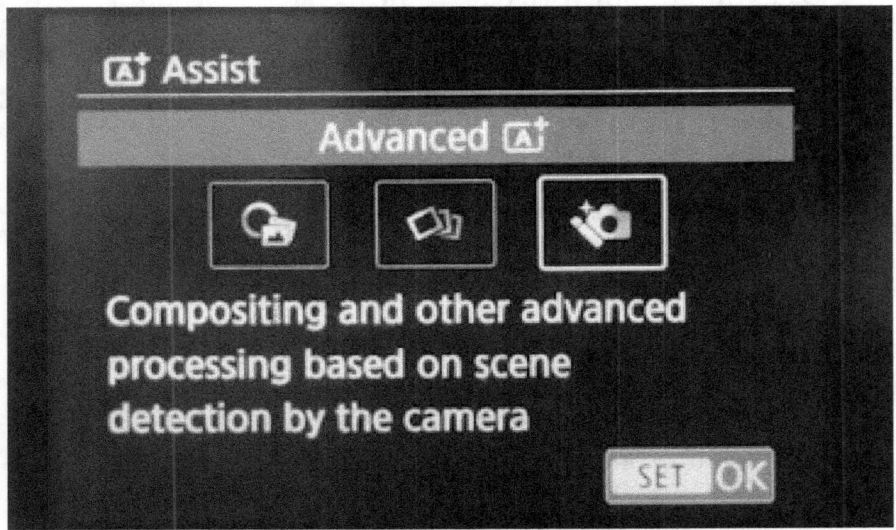

The second row in the figure has different Presets, like Vivid, Soft, and Warm, and colors like Green, Lime, Peach, Blue, and Purple. When you choose one of the seven special effects, a screen shows up with settings for that effect.

With Creative Assist, you can change your image's appearance by adjusting brightness, contrast, color richness, and color bias (amber/blue or green/magenta). You can also control the background blur to make it sharper or blurrier, affecting the depth of field.

If you change your camera's settings in Creative Assist mode, they'll be lost when you exit or turn off the camera. If you want to keep those settings for later, go to the Shooting 4 menu and select Retain Creative Assist Data. Remember, this option is only visible when the Mode Dial is set to SCN. Also, you can't use Background Blur with electronic flash.

Special Scene Mode

Turning the Mode Dial to SCN on the R50 camera activates the Special Scene mode. This mode offers 13 categories for common subjects you can photograph. Rotate the Mode Dial, then press Q/SET to select a Scene mode from the options displayed in the figure.

- **Portrait:** This setting uses bigger lens openings and quicker photo-taking times, giving you blurry backgrounds and clear pictures without shaky camera effects. If you keep the button pressed, the R50 will take many photos in a row, which is handy for catching quick facial expressions in portraits. Skin tones and hair look smoother and more attractive.

- **Group Photo:** Use a wide-angle lens to get great photos where everyone in a group looks sharp. It helps keep both people in the front and those in the back in focus by increasing the depth of field.

- **Landscape:** The R50 aims to have more focus by using smaller camera openings, and it enhances colors a bit for richer images. The built-in flash won't work, but it will flash if you connect and turn on an external Speedlite.

- **Panoramic Shot:** To make a wide photo, just turn your camera while taking the picture following the on-screen instructions.

- **Sports:** In this setting, the R50 camera aims to capture fast movements by using quick shutter speeds. It also lets you take pictures in a row with just one button press and stays focused on a moving subject using AI Servo AF. Check Chapter 5 for more details on autofocus choices.

- **Kids:** This mode helps the camera focus on active kids by continuously adjusting and taking many photos in a row. It also makes skin tones look lively. Aim the center point at your main subject, half-press the shutter button, and the camera will refocus to follow the child's movement. If it can't focus well, a blinking indicator in the viewfinder will let you know.

- **Panning:** In simple terms, this mode makes things look like they're moving using a slow shutter speed. When you move the camera while taking a picture, it creates a blurry effect that shows the motion of a subject.

- **Close-Up:** This mode is like a portrait setting but is better for close-up shots. It has wide f/stops to focus on your subjects and high shutter speeds to prevent shaky photos up close. If your camera is on a tripod or has image stabilization, try Aperture-priority (Av) mode for more control over depth-of-field with a smaller f/stop.

- **Food:** This mode makes your food pictures look bright and tasty with vibrant colors and strong contrast.

- **Night Portrait:** Mixes flash and natural light to create a photo where the main light comes from the flash, but the surrounding light lights the background. This mode requires longer exposures, so a tripod, monopod, or IS lens is necessary.

- **Handheld Night Scene:** In this setting, the R50 camera captures four photos and blends them to create a clear picture while minimizing shaky camera effects.

- **HDR Backlight Control:** The R50 camera clicks three pictures in a row, each with different brightness levels, and then puts them together to make one photo that shows more details in both bright and dark areas.

- **Silent Shutter:** Takes a quiet picture using the electronic shutter instead of the noisy mechanical shutter.

Creative Filters

The R50 lets you add cool filters to your photos while taking them. You can also use these filters on pictures you've already taken through the Playback menu. Applying filters while shooting lets you see how they'll look beforehand, and applying them later saves a new version of the photo without changing the original.

You can use cool photo effects on your camera. Just turn the Mode Dial to Creative Filters, press Q/SET, and pick from options like Black and White, Soft Focus, Fish-eye, and more. You can adjust settings for most effects, except for HDR modes, which only let you change Drive mode. Easy, right?

You can change how things look in five out of six options. Just use the up button and left/right controls to make them darker or lighter: Grainy B/W (Contrast), Soft Focus, Fish-eye (Strength), Water Painting (Color Density), and Toy Camera (Warm, Neutral, Cool colors).

Selecting a Shooting Mode

In Creative Zone modes, you can easily adjust settings like shutter speed and aperture to capture photos in different ways. Press the shutter button to clear the displayed shooting mode info when you turn the Mode dial.

P: Program AE

The camera changes how fast it takes a picture and the opening size based on its brightness. P means "Program," and Auto Exposure is called AE.

1. Turn the Mode dial to <P>.

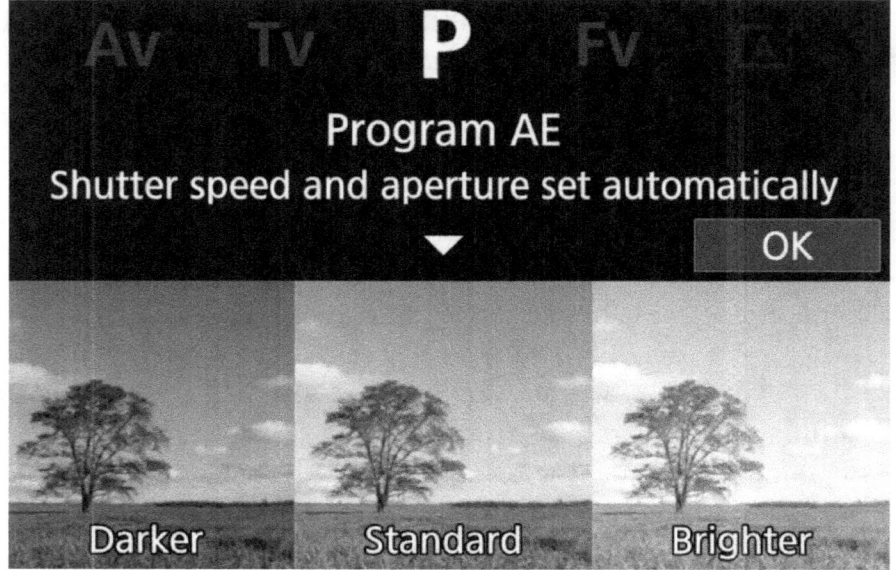

2. Focus on your subject by putting the AF point above it and halfway pressing the shutter until it turns green.

3. Check the display; if the exposure value isn't flashing, you can use a standard exposure.

4. Take the picture by fully pressing the shutter button after setting up your shot.

Note:

- If your camera shows blinking at "30" shutter speed and the smallest aperture, it means the photo is too dark.

- Use flash or raise the ISO.

- The photo is too bright if blinking occurs at "1/4000" shutter speed and the largest aperture.

- Lower the ISO or use an ND filter (sold separately) to reduce light.

Differences between <P> and <A+> modes

The <A+> mode helps prevent blurry photos by limiting some options and choosing settings like autofocus and metering for you. On the other hand, the P mode lets you manually adjust things like autofocus and metering while the camera automatically sets the shutter speed and aperture.

Program shift

In "P" mode, you can freely adjust the camera's shutter speed and aperture settings while keeping the exposure constant. This is called Program Shift. To do this, halfway press the shutter button and turn the mode dial until you see the desired settings on the screen. The program change ends automatically when the metering timer runs out, and you can't use Flash during Program Shift.

TV: Shutter Priority AE

In this setting, you pick how fast the camera takes a picture, and the camera figures out the right amount of light by adjusting the lens opening. Use a quick shutter speed (like 1/2000 sec) to capture a fast-moving scene. It freezes the action. If you use a slower speed (like 1/30 sec), you might get a blurry effect, showing the sense of motion in the picture.

1. Pick "TV" on the Mode dial.

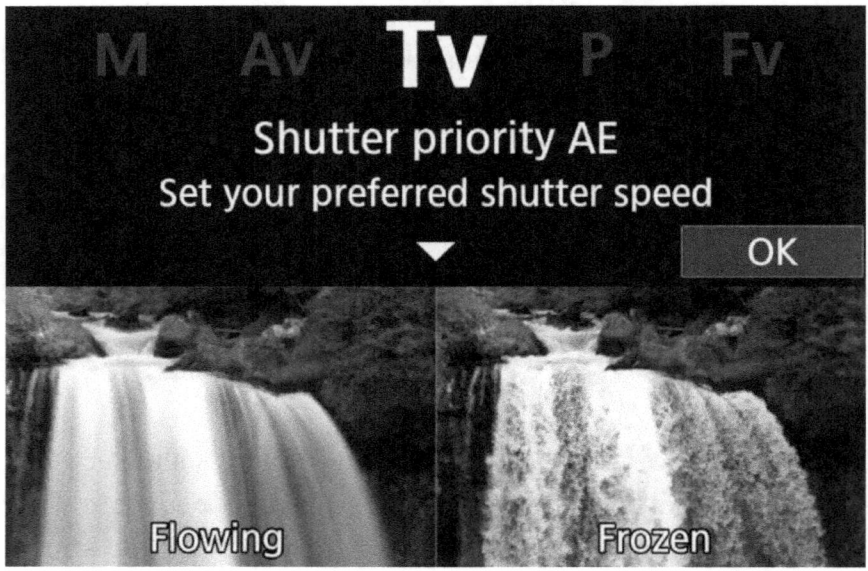

2. Adjust the shutter speed by turning the dial.

3. Half-press the shutter button to focus on your subject; the camera handles the aperture.

4. Look at the screen and take your shot. Make sure the aperture value isn't flashing for proper exposure.

AV: Aperture Priority AE

In this mode, the camera picks the right shutter speed, and you choose the aperture to get a well-exposed picture matching the subject's brightness.

- Blurry background: Use a small aperture like f/5.6.

- Sharp background and foreground: Set a large aperture like f/32.

1. Turn the Mode dial to "Av."

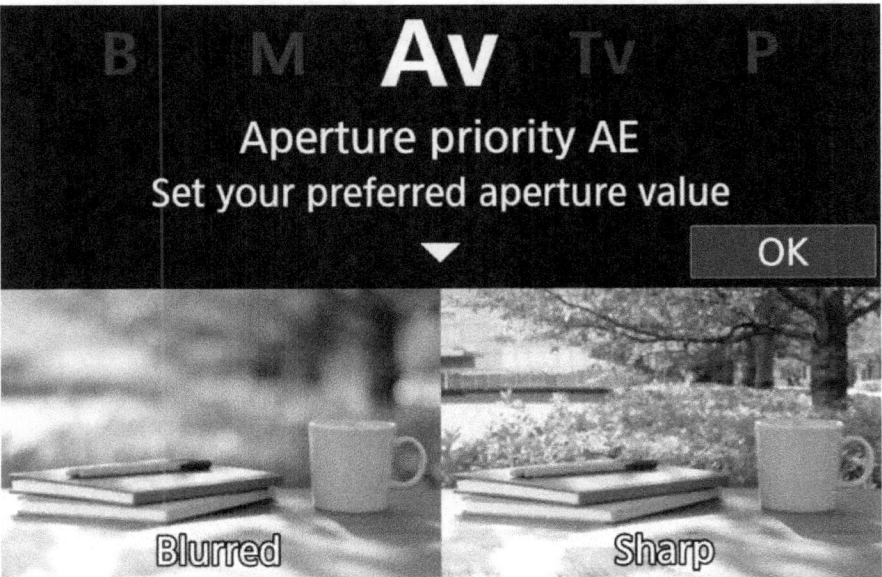

2. Pick the aperture you like.

3. Focus on your subject, press the shutter button halfway, and let the camera set the speed.

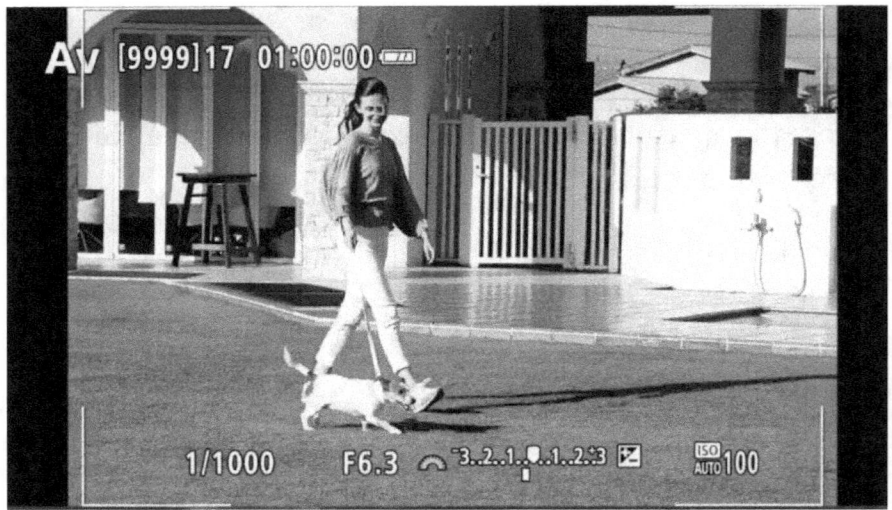

4. Look at the display, and if the shutter speed isn't blinking, you can take the shot for a standard exposure.

M: Manual Exposure

Choose the opening size and how long the camera stays open here.

1. Turn the Mode dial to set M.

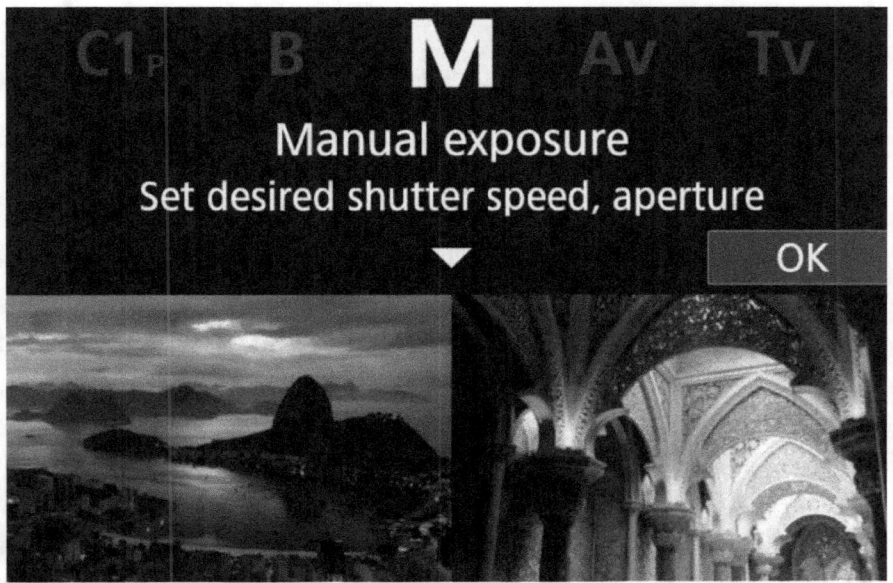

2. Use the <ISO> button to set the ISO speed.

3. Configure exposure compensation with ISO Auto.

4. Choose the shutter speed by turning the mode dial.

5. Press the up-arrow key and select an aperture value using the mode dial.

6. Focus on the subject and half-press the shutter button.

7. Check the exposure level mark to see if it's on target.

8. Adjust the shutter speed and aperture, then take the photo.

Long (Bulb) Exposures

In this mode, when you press and hold the shutter button, the camera keeps taking a photo for as long as you hold the button down. Here's how to do it:

1. Turn the Mode dial to M.

2. Choose [BULB] for the shutter speed by turning the mode dial to the left.

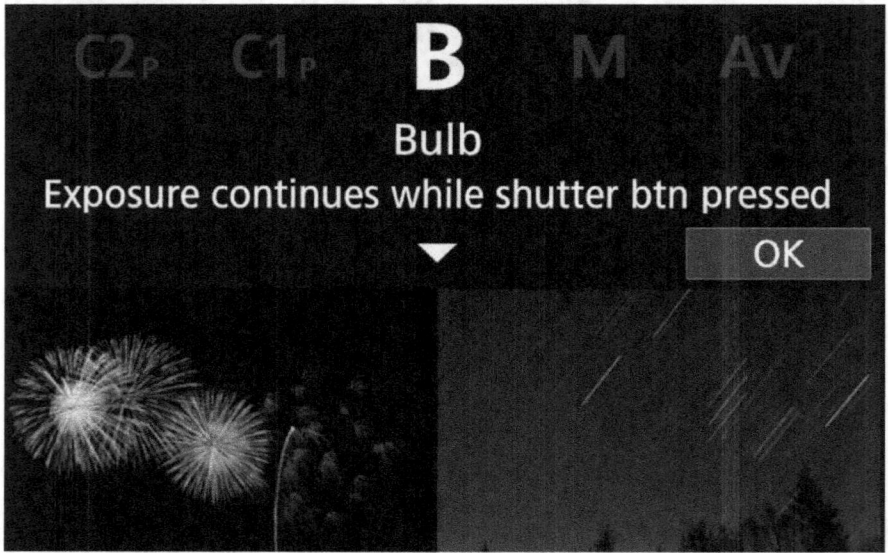

3. Pick your preferred aperture by pressing the up-arrow key and turning the mode dial.

4. Press and hold the shutter button to capture the image; the camera will keep exposing as long as you hold the button, and the elapsed time is shown on the LCD.

Don't point the camera at bright lights like the sun to prevent damage to the camera parts. Also, long exposures with bulbs make photos noisier than usual.

Choosing a Metering Mode

The Canon EOS R50 camera's main job is to expose your photos correctly. It does this by measuring the amount of light in a scene and adjusting the camera settings accordingly, which is called metering. The camera also has exposure compensation, so you can manually tweak the settings to deal with tricky lighting situations like strong backlight or deep shadows.

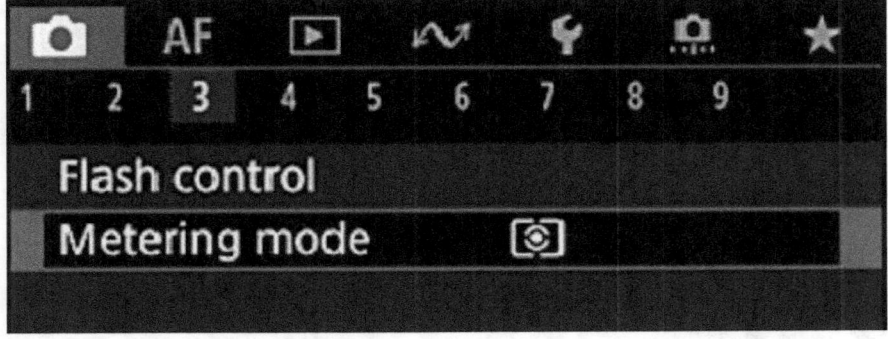

Select a metering mode on your Canon EOS R50 by going to the camera's menu or control panel. This mode helps the camera choose the right exposure settings for your photos. Remember, metering is just part of getting the right exposure; other settings like aperture, shutter speed, and ISO also play a role. Adjust these settings as needed, especially in tricky lighting situations like backlit photos or high-contrast scenes. Sometimes, the camera's usual settings might struggle to capture all the different shades in a scene, causing some parts to be too bright or dark. You can adjust exposure settings by using exposure compensation or different metering modes to fix this. You might also need to tweak the ISO or aperture for the best results.

Evaluative (or matrix) metering

The Canon EOS R50 camera has a common metering mode called evaluative or matrix metering. This mode looks at the brightness and contrast across the picture to determine the best exposure settings. It divides the scene into different zones, checks the brightness and contrast in each zone, and then picks the right exposure settings for the whole scene, not just a part.

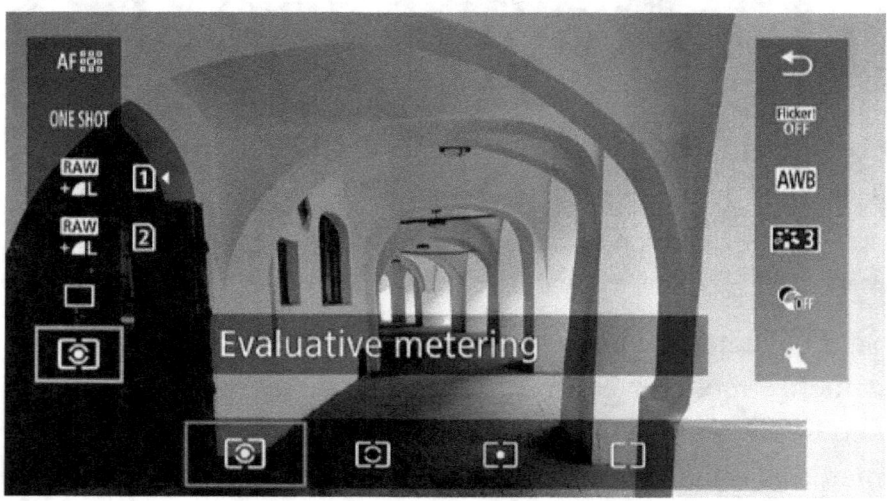

When you take pictures of bright and dark areas, like landscapes or portraits in sunlight, using "Evaluative" metering on the Canon EOS R50 helps ensure the whole photo looks good. Select this mode in the camera settings, and it will determine the right exposure by looking at different parts of the scene.

Evaluative metering helps you take well-exposed photos in different situations, but it's not always the best. In some cases, using spot or center-weighted metering may be better. For example, evaluative metering might make the camera underexpose of a person's face against a bright background. In such situations, spot metering is better to ensure the face is exposed correctly.

Just like this, using evaluative metering might make your camera make the subject too dark when taking a photo with a bright background. In this case, using center-weighted metering could be better because it considers the brightness in the middle of the frame, ensuring the subject is properly lit. Your choice of metering mode depends on the shooting situation and your preferences. Experimenting with different metering modes helps determine the best one for different scenarios and subjects.

Partial metering

In photography, metering plays a critical role in determining the appropriate exposure settings for a given scene. When you're focusing on a particular part of the picture, like a person's face or a bright object, partial metering becomes a valuable tool in refining the exposure calculations to precisely match the characteristics of that specific area.

Partial metering involves the camera analyzing the brightness and contrast within a defined portion of the frame, typically the middle 6.5 percent. This region is strategically chosen to include the primary subject or focal point of interest, providing a more accurate reading for exposure adjustments. By concentrating on this specific area, the camera assesses the light and shadow values, ensuring that the exposure is optimized for the targeted subject rather than being influenced by the overall scene.

For instance, when photographing a person's face against a backdrop of varying light conditions, partial metering helps the camera prioritize the subject's facial features. This is particularly beneficial in scenarios where the background might be considerably brighter or darker than the subject. By considering only the middle portion of the frame, partial metering ensures that the exposure settings are tailored to the nuances of the focal point, preventing overexposure or underexposure caused by extreme variations in lighting.

Moreover, when dealing with high-contrast scenes where there are both bright and dark areas, partial metering allows for a more balanced and nuanced exposure. The camera intelligently evaluates the brightness values in the selected region, providing a more accurate representation of the targeted subject while maintaining details in both highlight and shadow areas.

Spot metering

The Canon EOS R50 camera has a feature called "spot metering" that lets you precisely measure the exposure of a small part of the picture. In this mode, the camera checks the brightness of a small circle in the center of the frame (about 1% to 5% of the whole frame). It is handy to ensure a specific area, like a person's face or a small object, is well-lit. You can also use it to create cool effects by intentionally making some parts darker or brighter.

Follow these steps to use spot metering on the Canon EOS R50 camera:

1. Go to your camera settings and turn on spot metering.

2. Use the joystick or touch screen to select the part of the frame you want to measure.

3. Half-press the shutter button to activate the exposure metering. The camera will measure the brightness of the selected area and set the exposure accordingly.

4. Adjust exposure settings using exposure compensation, auto exposure bracketing, or manual adjustments for the perfect exposure.

Using spot metering on your camera can be tricky compared to other modes. You must be precise in placing the metering area and may need to adjust settings more often. Learn how your camera's metering works, consider lighting and practice using spot metering effectively in different situations.

When you use spot metering, pay attention to parts of the picture that are much brighter or darker than the spot you picked. If your subject is against a bright background, the camera might not expose it correctly. You might need to adjust the exposure or use exposure compensation to get the right result.

Highlight Weighted Metering

The Canon EOS R50 camera has a cool feature called Highlight Weighted Metering. It helps your camera measure exposure more accurately by focusing on the bright parts in your shot. This is handy because it prevents overexposure and ensures important details in those bright areas are captured well. If you want to learn more about how it works and when to use it, keep reading!

In "Highlight Weighted Metering," your camera emphasizes the brightest parts of the scene when setting exposure. This means it focuses on the brightest areas in your photo rather than the overall brightness. This is especially useful in high-contrast situations with both bright highlights and dark shadows.

If you want to capture bright details in your photo, Highlight Weighted Metering can help. It's useful when shooting against bright backgrounds, like a sunny sky or a bright object against a dark background. This metering mode ensures your highlights aren't too bright while still capturing details in darker areas, resulting in a more balanced and appealing photo with better exposure and detail.

To make your Canon EOS R50 focus more on bright areas in your photos, go to the camera settings, select Highlight Weighted Metering, and prioritize highlights by choosing it in the Metering Mode menu accessed through the "Q" button.

Instead of adjusting exposure for the overall brightness of a scene, Highlight Weighted Metering adjusts based on the brightest parts of your photo. Keep in mind that it might not always give the best exposure. You might prefer other metering modes like Evaluative or Center-Weighted Average Metering depending on your lighting and composition.

Center-weighted average metering

The Canon EOS R50 camera has a mode called center-weighted metering. In simple terms, when setting the exposure, this mode pays extra attention to the middle of the picture but still considers the overall lighting in the entire frame. It focuses more on the center area when measuring the light for the whole scene.

Photographers often use center-weighted metering when taking pictures with the subject in the center and a consistent background brightness. This is common in still life, studio, and portrait photography, where the background is usually neutral or controlled. Consider the size and position of the metering area, which on the Canon EOS R5 defaults to a middle circle covering about 12% of the frame. You can adjust the metering area to fit your specific needs.

You can adjust the metering area on the Canon EOS R50 camera by selecting "center-weighted average + AF point" or "center-weighted average" mode in the menu. Use the joystick to move the metering area where you want it. Additionally, you can customize the metering area size by assigning it to a camera control knob in the custom controls menu. Remember the subject's and overall scene brightness when using center-weighted metering to avoid overexposed or underexposed images. In challenging lighting conditions, like low light or high contrast situations, center-weighted metering can be useful, and you may need to adjust exposure compensation or switch the metering mode accordingly.

Use center-weighted metering when you want the main subject well-lit while considering the surroundings. But remember, it might not be the best choice every time. Depending on lighting and subject, evaluative or spot metering might be better. Spot metering focuses on one point, while evaluative metering looks at the whole scene. For specific situations like backlighting, spot metering can be useful.

Exposure compensation

Exposure compensation allows you to adjust how bright or dark your camera takes pictures. It's useful when your subject is in front of a bright background, as it helps make sure your photo looks right, even if the camera's automatic settings might not get it perfect.

Highlight tone priority

Highlight tone priority helps keep details in bright parts of a photo. When you turn it on, the camera uses a lower ISO and a wider range to capture more info in the highlights.

Auto Lighting Optimizer

This tool makes photos look better by adjusting how bright and clear they are. It's useful for fixing pictures with uneven lighting or a mix of bright and dark areas.

Choosing the right metering mode might involve trying different ones, but here are some simple rules to help: spot and partial metering are good for focusing on specific parts of a scene, evaluative metering works well for most situations, and center-weighted average metering is useful for subjects in the center of the frame, like in portrait photos. There are four metering modes to measure brightness, with evaluative metering often recommended, especially in the Basic Zone, where it's automatically set.

Choosing a Drive Mode

You can pick between single-drive and continuous-drive options. Press the right arrow key and turn the dial to choose the driving mode that fits the environment or object.

Single shooting

In the single shooting mode, the camera is set to take a solitary photograph each time the shutter button is pressed. This deliberate and controlled approach to capturing images is ideal for situations where precision, careful composition, and thoughtful timing are paramount. By pressing the shutter button once, photographers can ensure that they capture a specific moment without the risk of rapid-fire shots that might lead to unintentional redundancy or missed opportunities.

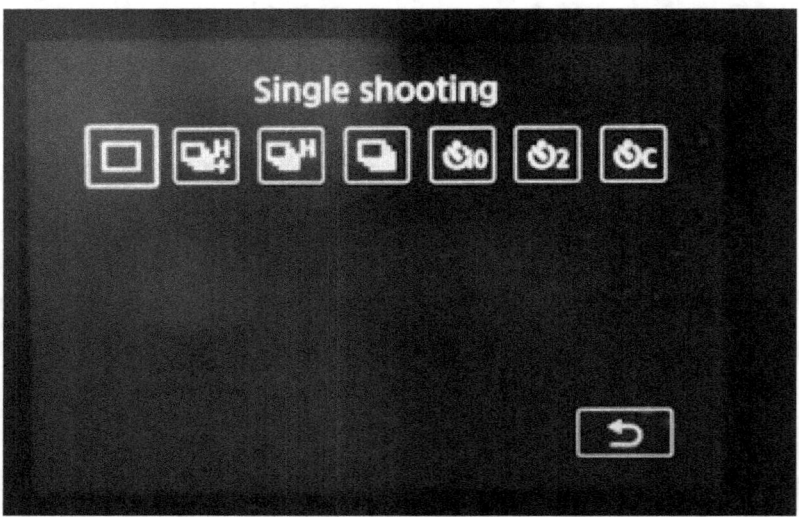

Single shooting is particularly advantageous in scenarios where the subject is static, and the photographer seeks to capture a single, decisive moment. This mode is commonly used in portrait photography, still life, landscape photography, and other situations where the primary objective is to create a well-composed and singular image. By taking only one shot at a time, photographers have the opportunity to fine-tune their composition, adjust focus, and make any necessary exposure adjustments between each frame.

This shooting mode is also favored when working in environments with limited storage capacity, as it prevents the rapid accumulation of numerous images. Photographers may prefer single shooting when they aim for a more thoughtful and intentional approach to their craft, emphasizing quality over quantity.

High-speed continuous shooting +

You can take pictures quickly by holding down the shutter button depending on how you set the Shutter mode.

- [Electronic]: up to 15 shots per second.

- [Elec. 1st-curtain]: up to approximately 12 shots per second.

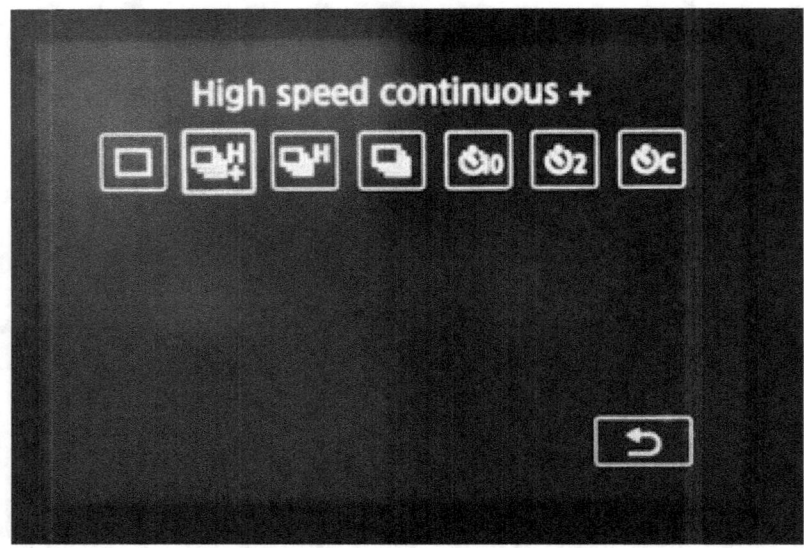

Setting Resolution and File Type (The Image Quality Setting)

Adjusting the Image Quality setting

When you take pictures with the Canon EOS R50 camera, how good the photos look and how much editing you need depends on the image quality. You can adjust the camera's Image Settings menu to match your preferences.

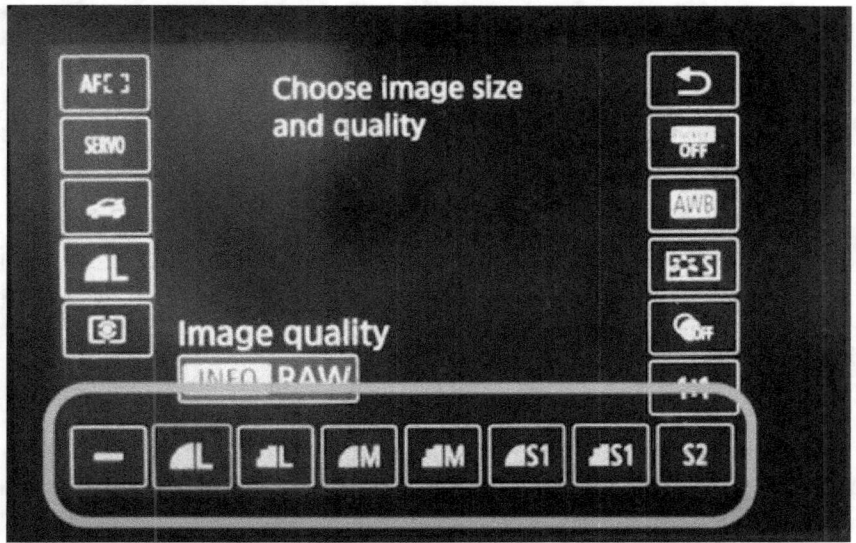

Consider these important settings when adjusting the image quality on your Canon EOS R5 camera:

1. **Image Quality:** This setting controls how sharp and compact your photos are. You can pick large, top-notch RAW files or smaller, compressed JPEG files. Professionals often choose RAW for flexibility, even though it uses more storage than JPEG.

2. **Picture Style:** Pick different looks for your photos with Picture Styles. Each style has its contrast, saturation, and sharpness settings, letting you create various effects or match specific shooting conditions. Portrait, Landscape, and Standard are some common styles to choose from.

3. **Auto Lighting Optimizer:** To make your photos look better, you can use the Auto Lighting Optimizer. It

automatically adjusts the brightness and contrast of your pictures, which is handy when taking photos in tricky lighting, like when the background is too bright or there's a big difference between light and dark areas.

4. **Highlight Tone Priority:** Reducing highlight clipping with the Highlight Tone Priority helps keep details in bright areas of your photos, especially useful in bright and high-contrast scenes or when capturing things like the sky or reflective surfaces.

5. **Long exposure noise reduction:** If your photos have too much-unwanted graininess (noise) because you took them with a long exposure, you can fix that. Use Long Exposure Noise Reduction – it works by taking a second picture with the lens covered to capture only the noise, reducing that noise from your original photo. It is handy for cleaner, smoother images, especially in low-light situations.

6. **High ISO Speed Noise Reduction:** If you take pictures in low light or use high ISO settings, your photos might have unwanted noise. The High ISO Speed Noise Reduction option helps reduce this noise automatically, giving you cleaner and smoother photographs.

7. **Lens Aberration Correction:** To make sure your photos look great and avoid unwanted issues like color distortion, bending, and dark edges, just turn on Lens Aberration Correction. It helps your camera fix these common lens problems automatically. Also, play around with the image settings to customize how your photos

look, giving you more control and a better understanding of your camera.

Remember, some camera settings impact picture quality more than others, and certain settings work better in specific shooting conditions. For example, in fast-paced situations, you might not need Long Exposure Noise Reduction, and Highlight Tone Priority might not be useful in low-contrast settings.

To achieve the desired effects in your photos, consider adjusting the settings on your camera and think about post-processing. RAW files offer flexibility and can be customized using programs like Adobe Lightroom or Capture One. You have choices for pixel count and picture quality, deciding between RAW or other image quality options for your photographs.

1. Pick how good you want the picture to be.

2. Adjust the imge quality.

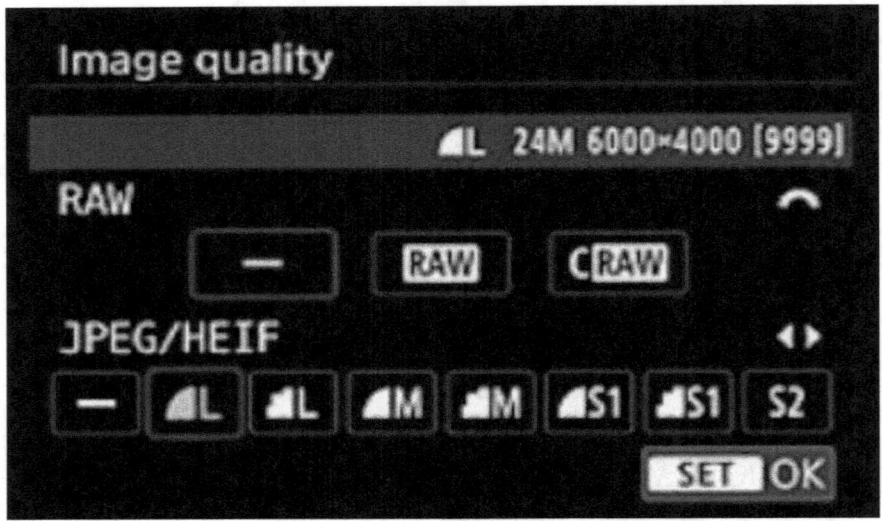

Understanding file type (JPEG or Raw)

RAW Image

Improve your photos and get the best image quality using the advanced options on the Canon EOS R50 camera. Let's explore some important settings for RAW images on the Canon EOS R50.

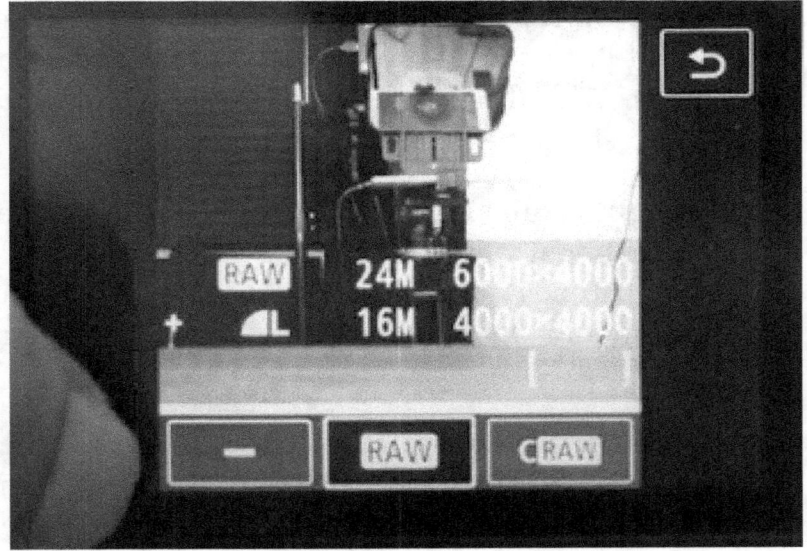

1. **RAW Image Type:** The Canon EOS R5 has two types of RAW image formats: Uncompressed RAW, which gives lots of detail and flexibility for editing, and CRAW (Compressed RAW), which has smaller file sizes, making it easier to store and share, but with a bit less detail.

2. **Bit Depth:** The Canon EOS R50 can capture high-quality RAW photos at either 14-bit or 12-bit depths. Choosing 14-bit gives experts more color and tone flexibility during editing, while 12-bit is handy when dealing with smaller file sizes or faster transmission, although with slightly less editing flexibility.

3. **White Balance:** The Canon EOS R50 lets you choose white balance manually or use preset options. After taking a RAW photo, the white balance setting is saved, but you can still adjust it later when editing the picture.

4. **Picture Style:** The Canon EOS R50 lets you choose different Picture Styles to change how your photos look and feel. With these styles, you can adjust things like contrast, sharpness, and saturation.

5. **Highlight Tone Priority:** This feature helps keep details in bright areas with a strong contrast. Turning on Highlight Tone Priority makes the camera capture more highlight info but might slightly reduce the overall contrast.

6. **Auto Lighting Optimizer:** This tool helps improve brightness and clarity in different lighting. When turned on, the camera looks at the scene, adjusts brightness, and fine-tunes contrast for a better picture.

7. **Long Exposure Noise Reduction:** This tool helps reduce unwanted fuzziness in photos taken with a long exposure. When turned on, the camera takes a second photo the same way but with the shutter closed. It uses this dark image to minimize noise in the first photo.

8. **High ISO Noise Reduction:** This tool can help reduce unwanted grain in photos taken with high ISO settings. When turned on, the camera works to reduce noise in the picture.

9. **Lens Aberration Correction:** It's a tool that fixes how pictures look, like bending, color problems, and dark corners. The camera uses it to make the photo look better when turned on. Remember, when you take pictures in RAW format, the camera doesn't fix them automatically. You need software like Adobe Lightroom

or Capture One later to make the picture look the way you want. Even though it gives you more control, it requires more effort and skill. The RAW format has advantages, like adjusting brightness and bringing out details in shadows and highlights.

With RAW photos, you can easily change exposure, contrast, and brightness after taking the picture without losing quality. The RAW format lets you adjust white balance and color temperature during editing without introducing noise or other issues.

When taking pictures in RAW format, it's important to carefully check the histogram on your camera's display. RAW photos contain unprocessed data from the image sensor and can be edited using software like Digital Photo Professional. You can adjust the photos differently and save them as JPEG, HEIF, or other formats based on your preferences.

RAW Image Processing

Edit your photos the way you want using the Canon EOS R50's editing tools for RAW images. Check out some important RAW processing options on the Canon EOS R50.

- **Picture Style:** Using the Picture Style feature, you can adjust how your photos look. Different styles include Standard, Portrait, Landscape, Neutral, Faithful, and Monochrome. Each style offers various settings for contrast, sharpness, color tone, and saturation, allowing you to customize your photos based on what you like.

99

- **White Balance:** You can change the colors in your photos by using White Balance. It helps correct color issues or give a specific look. Options like Auto, Daylight, Shade, Cloudy, Tungsten, White Fluorescent Light, Flash, and Custom are available.

- **Exposure Compensation:** Adjusting Exposure Compensation lets you make your photos brighter or darker by up to +/- 5 stops. It's useful for fixing exposure issues or achieving a specific look in your pictures.

- **Highlight Tone Priority:** In bright situations, using Highlight Tone Priority can keep details in the bright areas of your photos. Turning it on adjusts the exposure to save those bright details, making the overall photo slightly darker.

- **High ISO Noise Reduction:** Choose different settings to make high ISO photos look cleaner. You can pick from options like Off, Low, Standard, High, and Multi Shot Noise Reduction for noise reduction.

- **Lens Aberration Correction:** This tool helps fix lens issues, like color problems, dark edges, and distortion, especially for wide-angle or strongly problematic lenses.

Remember to use it when working with RAW photos because they offer more editing options and information than JPEGs. RAW lets you adjust exposure, white balance, and style without losing image quality, which is handy for fixing exposure or color mistakes.

Consider your workflow, as processing RAW photos requires a powerful computer and more storage than JPEGs. You'll also need specialized software like Adobe Photoshop or Lightroom.

Resizing JPEG/HEIF Images

You can make a JPEG or HEIF picture smaller by reducing its pixels and saving it as a new image. This resizing applies to RAW+JPEG and RAW+HEIF photos but not to pictures, RAW

photos, or frame grabs from 4K videos.

1. Pick Resize.

2. Look through your photos.

3. Use the arrow keys to select a picture to resize.

4. Choose the size you want.

5. Save it by clicking [OK].

6. Confirm the file number and folder, then select OK.

Cropping JPEG/HEIF Images

You can cut and save a part of a JPEG or HEIF picture. But you can't do that with RAW photos or frames from 4K videos.

1. Pick "Cropping."

2. Select an image using the arrow keys.

3. Choose a frame for your cropped picture. The cropped image will fit inside that frame.

Resizing the cropping frame size

You can make the cropping frame bigger or smaller by clicking the Magnify button. When you make the frame smaller, the cropped picture will look larger.

Correcting tilt

Adjust the picture tilt by +10 degrees. Choose the second option on the mode dial and press SET. Use the mode dial or the arrow buttons on the screen to fine-tune the tilt in increments (0.1° or 0.5°). Check the tilt against the grid, and when satisfied, press SET to save the corrections.

CHAPTER 5: CAPTURING VIDEO

Movie Shooting Menus

Movie Recording

Turn the Mode dial to the movie setting. Just press the movie shutter button while taking pictures to start recording movies.

Auto-exposure Movie

Automatic exposure control adjusts to the lighting conditions.

1. Set the Mode dial.

2. Select "Shooting mode."

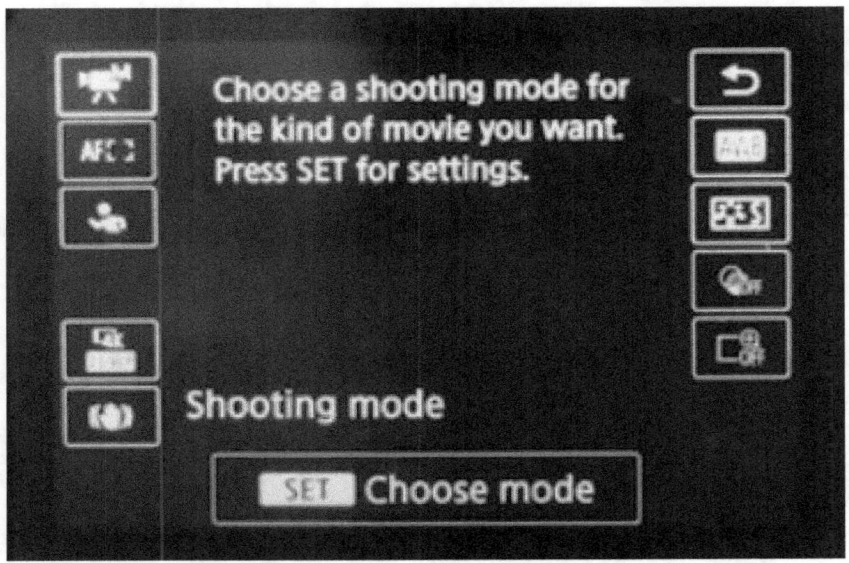

3. Choose "Movie auto exposure."

103

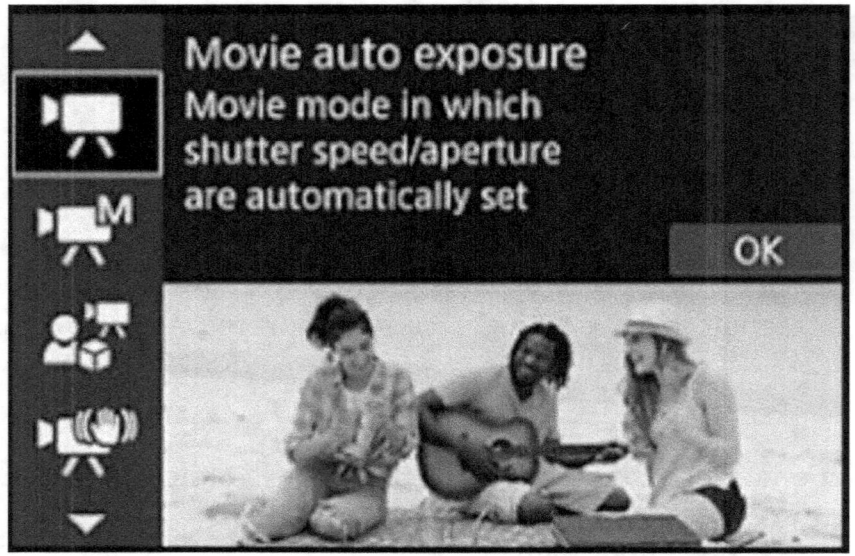

4. Focus on the subject using manual focus or AF before recording.

5. Press the movie shooting button to start recording.

Manual Exposure Movie

You can change the shutter speed, aperture size, and ISO speed while making videos.

1. Turn the Mode dial.

2. Pick "Shooting mode."

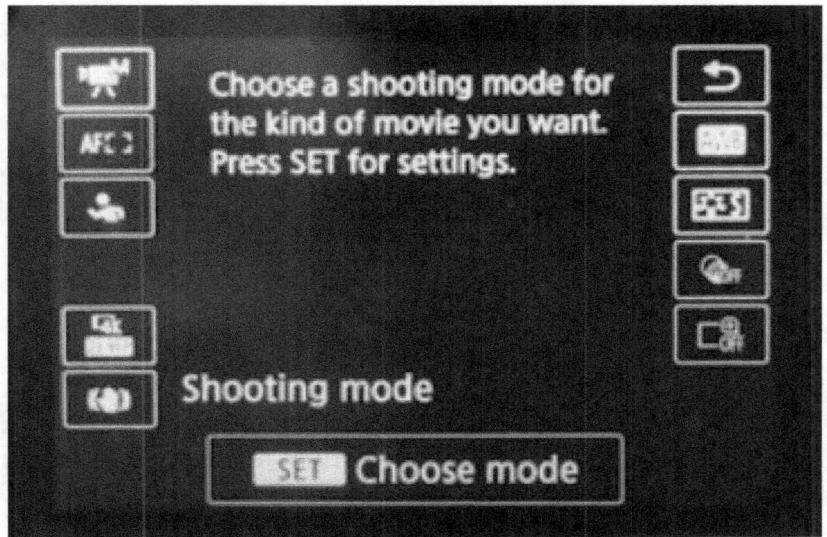

3. Select Movie manual exp.

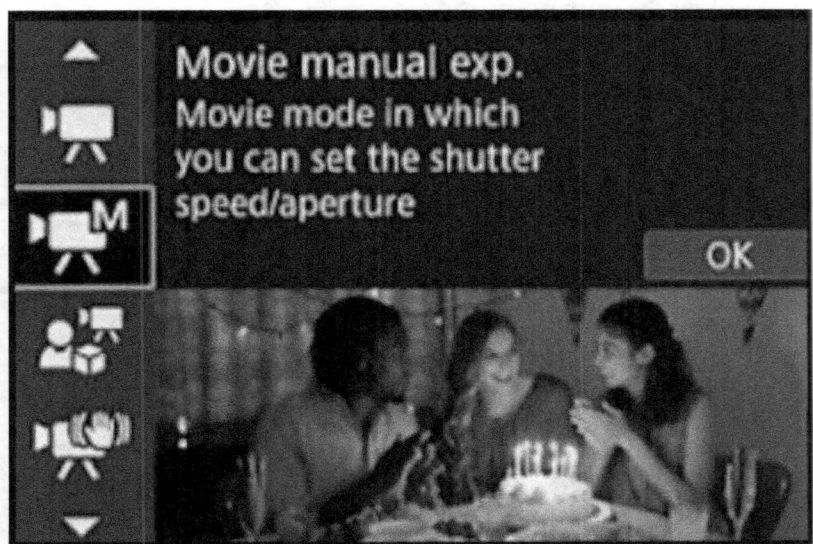

Set ISO, shutter speed, and aperture.

Check the exposure level halfway by pressing the shutter.

Use the arrow keys to adjust settings.

4. The <ISO> button changes ISO speed.

5. Record the Movie, paying attention.

Close-Up Demo Movie

Focus more on things close to the camera, especially in product evaluations and demonstrations.

1. Set the ModeMode dial to Movie mode.

2. Select "Shooting mode."

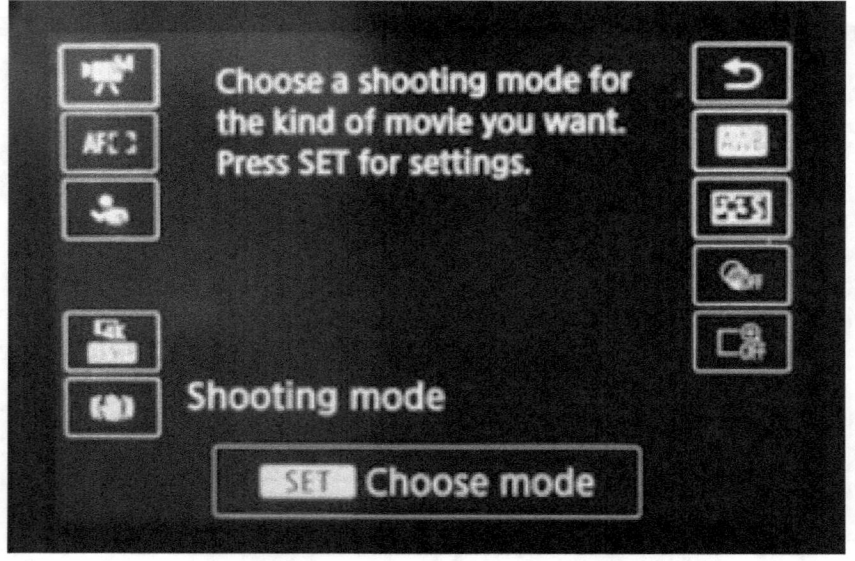

3. Pick a Movie for a close-up demonstration.

4. Record a close-up demo movie.

IS Mode Movie

When making movies, you can reduce camera shake. Even if you're using lenses without image stabilization (IS), you can still get decent stabilization. If you have an IS lens, turn on the stabilizer by setting it to <ON>.

1. Start by setting the mode dial to Movie mode.

2. Select "Shooting mode."

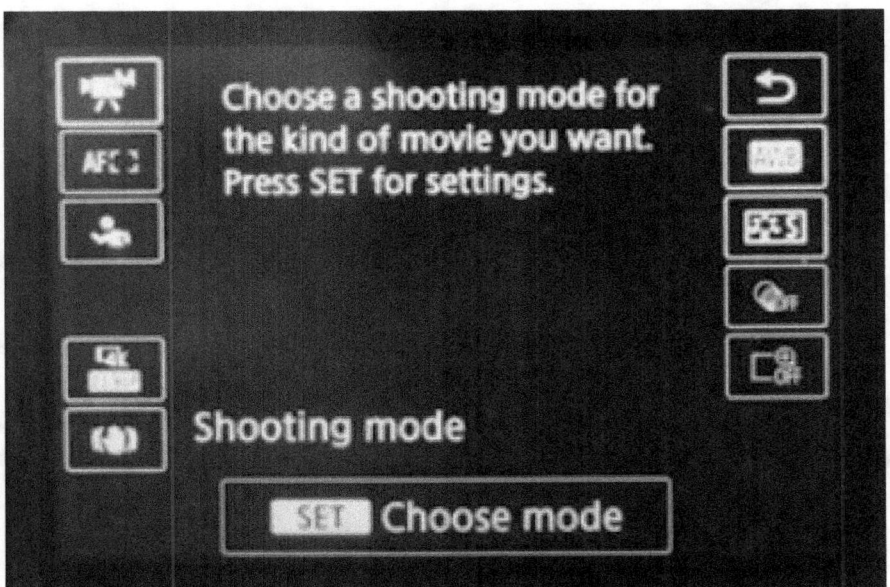

3. Choose "Movie IS mode."

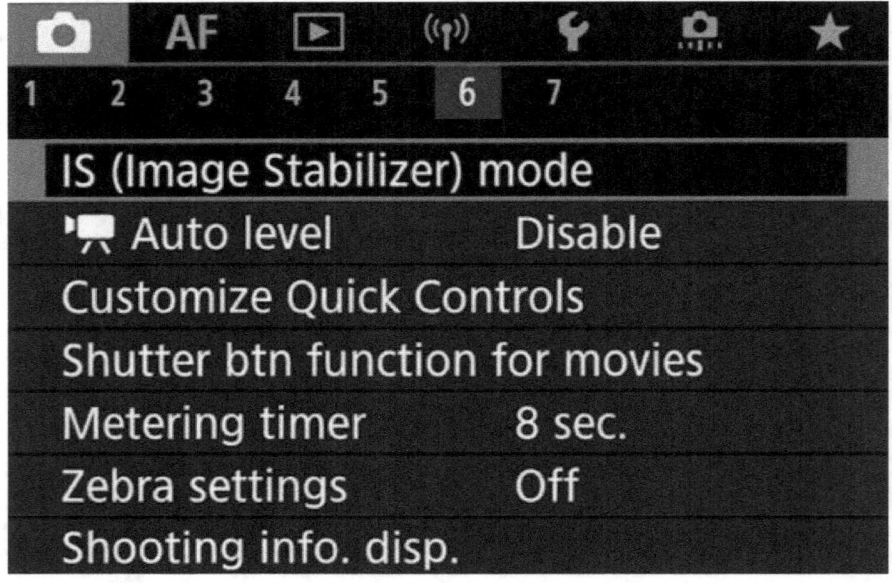

4. Pick a stabilization option, then press the * button to start.

- Turn off image stabilization for a standard view.

- Enable picture stabilization for a slightly enlarged picture.

- Opt for stronger image stabilization ([On] with enhanced) for further enlargement.

- Auto level maintains horizontal alignment during video recording.

5. Begin recording the Movie using the usual process.

HDR Movie Mode

High dynamic range movies show more details in bright areas during high-contrast scenes. To make one:

1. Set the ModeMode dial to Movie mode.

2. Select "Shooting mode."

3. Pick an HDR Movie.

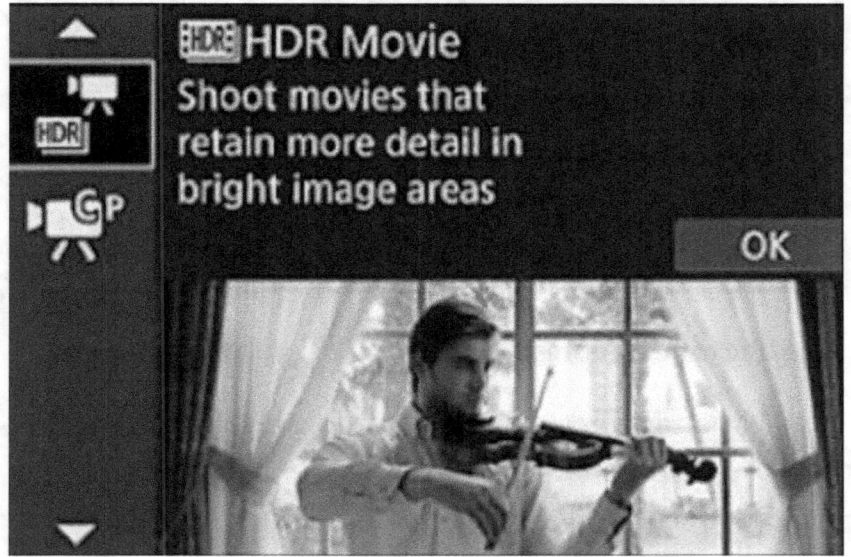

4. Record a video like you normally would for a regular movie.

Custom Shooting Mode

To record a video with your preferred settings, follow these steps:

1. Turn the mode dial to Movie mode.

2. Select "Shooting mode."

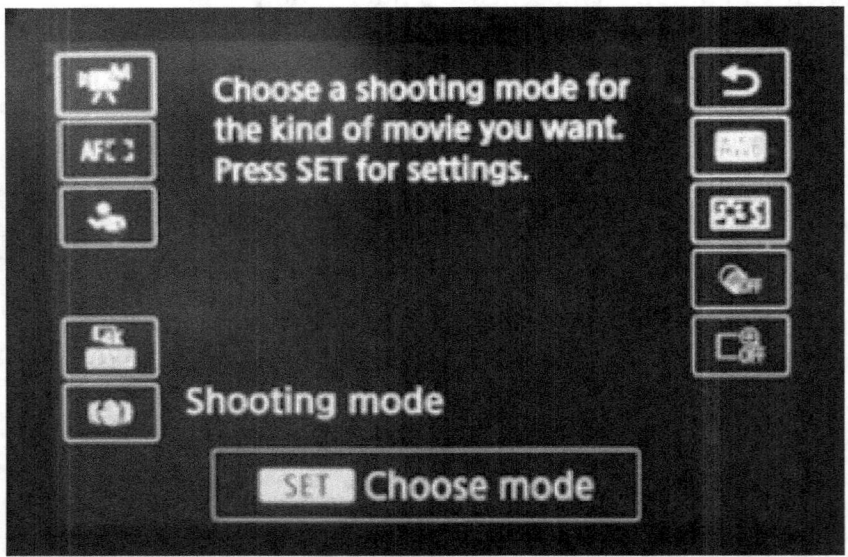

3. Pick the custom shooting mode.

4. Pay attention and begin recording the video.

Still Photo Shooting

You can't snap photos in video mode. Switch to a different mode on the dial to capture still pictures.

High Frame Rate

To capture slow-motion movies, use high frame rates like 119.9 or 100.0 frames per second. Just keep in mind there's a 15-minute limit for each movie recording.

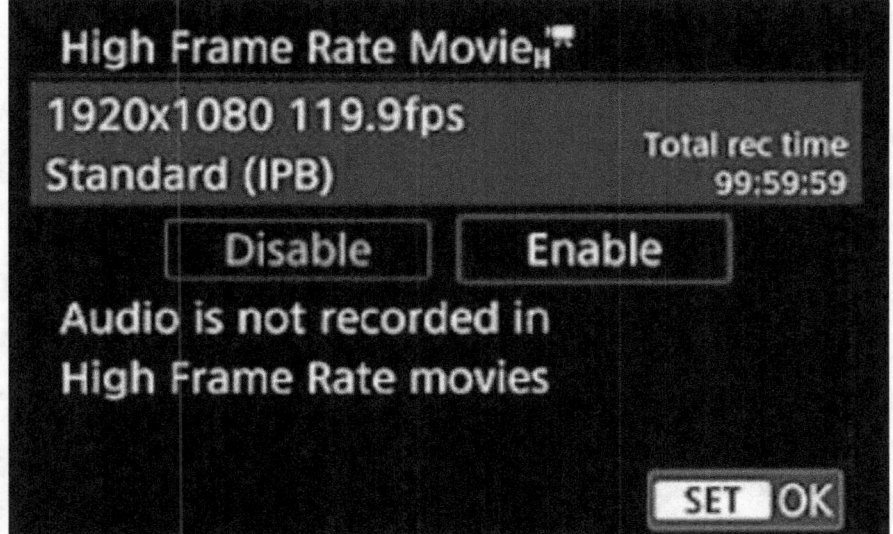

Sound Recording

You can record videos with sound using an external microphone or the one built into your device. You can also adjust the sound recording level using the Sound recording settings.

Built-in Microphone

The EOS R50 comes equipped with a stereo microphone for convenient and basic audio recording. It's suitable for everyday shooting where ambient sounds and clear dialogue are sufficient. However, limitations include:

- **Limited directionality:** The microphone picks up sound from all directions, potentially capturing unwanted background noise.

- **Lower audio quality**: The built-in microphone might not capture high-fidelity audio, especially for demanding projects or noisy environments.

External Microphone Options

For more professional sound recording, the EOS R50 offers several external microphone options:

- **3.5mm Microphone Jack:** This allows you to connect a directional microphone for improved audio clarity and focus. Directional mics isolate your subject's sound by minimizing background noise, ideal for interviews, vlogs, or nature documentaries.

- **Mic Input via Hot Shoe:** You can attach an external audio adapter to the camera's hot shoe, enabling connection of XLR microphones or other professional audio equipment. This provides the highest audio quality and control, perfect for serious videographers and filmmakers.

Sound Recording Features

The EOS R50 offers several features to enhance your sound recording experience:

- **Auto Gain Control (AGC):** This automatically adjusts the audio level to prevent distortion, especially helpful in fluctuating environments.

- **Manual Audio Level:** You can manually adjust the recording level for precise control, ensuring optimal sound capturing for your needs.

- **Wind Filter:** This reduces the impact of wind noise, beneficial when shooting outdoors.

- **Headphone Monitoring:** Connect headphones to the camera's 3.5mm jack to monitor the audio in real-time and ensure proper recording levels.

Sound Recording/Sound-Recording Level

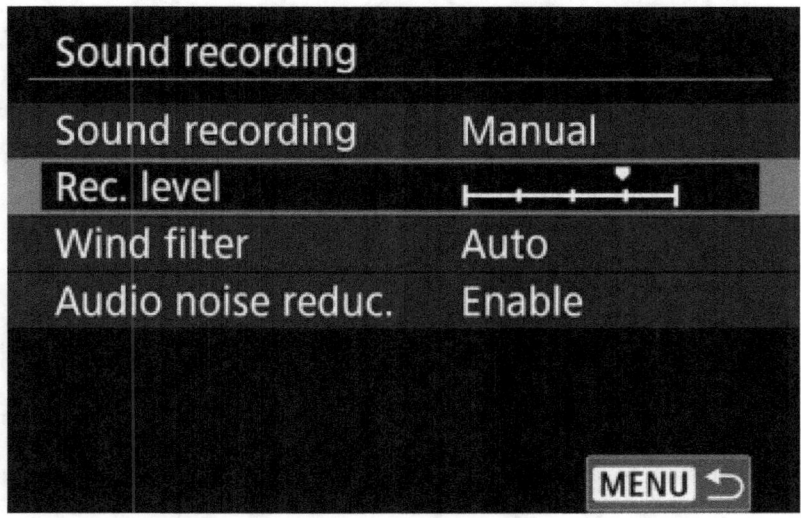

Auto

The recording volume adjusts by itself. It changes based on the loudness of the sound, thanks to the automatic level control.

Manual

You can adjust the recording volume by selecting "Rec. level" and using the arrow keys. Watch the level meter and, if needed, set the peak hold, so it occasionally lights up to the right of "12" (-12 dB) for loud sounds. Avoid going above "0" to prevent distortion.

Disable

No sound will be recorded.

Wind Filter

Select Auto to reduce wind noise in the audio. If you connect external microphones, the wind filter feature is turned off, causing a slight decrease in deep bass tones.

Compression, Resolution, and Frame Rates

I've shown you how to set things up and use them, focusing on the basics without diving into technical terms. This info will guide your choices. Even if you're not an expert in filming, the variety of choices like compression, resolution, and frame rates can be overwhelming. This section aims to make it clearer for you.

Compression

Let's talk about compression first. The camera saves files using the H.264/MPEG-4 method. When choosing Movie Size options, you can pick ALL-I or IPB compression (Standard or Light) for many of them.

- **ALL-I (All Intraframe):** When making time-lapse videos, there's a mode called ALL-I compression. It helps with editing by squeezing each frame before saving it to your memory card. It's like turning each shot into a smaller, easier-to-edit still image, even though it may not be the most efficient way to make files smaller.

- **IPB (Standard):** This is a new way of making video files smaller by saving only certain important frames and filling in the rest by guessing from nearby frames. It's called IPB, and Canon considers it a standard method. There are three types of frames: I-frames are complete frames, P-frames only save changes from the previous frame, and B-frames use differences from the previous and next frames. It makes the video files smaller, but the quality is lower and may need more processing power. If you use this method, you might need to convert your videos for editing, and it may not be the best choice for fast-moving scenes.

- **IPB (Light):** It records at a lower quality but makes smaller files faster to transfer, works on more devices, and allows longer recording. This option can be helpful if you don't need the best quality.

If you use a smaller SDHC card, the video files are limited to 4GB. When a file hits this limit, the camera starts a new one. You need to watch or combine these files separately.

But, if you use a larger SDXC card, files can be bigger than 4GB. Still, your computer might have some restrictions on handling such large files.

Resolution

The Canon EOS R50 offers multiple video resolution options, catering to different needs and output purposes. Resolution options are less technical.

- **4K (3840 × 2160):** This super clear format is the future, even though there aren't many options for content and displays right now. As you get more into videos, you might end up recording a lot in 4K, even if you plan to share Full HD videos. Some editors believe that 4K videos converted to Full HD look better than videos originally recorded in Full HD.

- **Full HD (1920 × 1080):** This resolution is called "full HD," it's the best quality when using HDTV. Most monitors and HD TVs can show this resolution, so use it for high-quality projects, especially if you're editing and making cool-looking DVDs.

Frame Rate

In the world of digital cameras, when shooting videos, you can easily choose frame rates. Forget about the confusing options like 50/25 fps and 60/30 fps—they are pairs of frame rates for different video standards. Use 60/30 fps in places like North America and Japan (following the NTSC standard), and use 50/25 fps in Europe, Russia, China, Africa, Australia, and other regions (following the PAL standard). If you're in India, just think in terms of 50/25 fps.

The third option is a standard movie rate of 24 frames per second (fps). Keep in mind that these rates are approximate. For example, a 24 fps setting gives you 23.976 frames per second. Video at 30 fps translates to 29.97 frames per second. The R50 camera's High Frame Rate option captures video at 119.99 fps, roughly 120 fps for NTSC and 100 fps for PAL. The difference comes down to the "worlds" of motion images – film (24 fps) and video (30 fps in NTSC regions). Editing software can handle both, and your choice depends on your video plans.

Filming at 24 frames per second (fps) gives your Movie a classic "film" look with fine details, but it might cause a jerky effect called "judder" for moving subjects or camera pans. On the other hand, 30 or 60 fps creates a smoother, less jittery home-video appearance on electronic monitors. Experiment with both frame rates to find what suits your preferences and video-editing software.

Another factor is the difference between a rolling shutter and a global shutter. Rolling shutter captures each line one after another, potentially causing a Jell-o-like effect with moving subjects. Global shutter in professional video cameras captures the entire frame simultaneously, avoiding this issue. If you don't have a global shutter, be aware of potential problems when shooting action scenes.

High Frame Rate Video

The High Frame Rate slow-motion video option lets you record movies that play back in slow motion, like in Baywatch. However, there are trade-offs: the video is in Standard HD resolution (1280 × 720), silent, and autofocus is disabled. It records at 120p (NTSC) or 100p (PAL) but plays back at 30/25 fps, making each frame last 4 times longer.

Remember there might be flickering under certain lights and issues when outputting to HDMI. Also, time codes aren't recorded in Free Run mode, so check your Movie Recording Size Setting after turning off the High Frame Rate video.

HDR Movies

HDR shooting makes your videos look better in bright and dark scenes. Just turn on HDR Shooting, select the right movie settings, and press the Q/SET button to enable HDR Movie Shooting. Your camera will merge frames to create a high-quality video with improved details in highlights and shadows. Experiment to find the best results and be aware of possible noise or distortion.

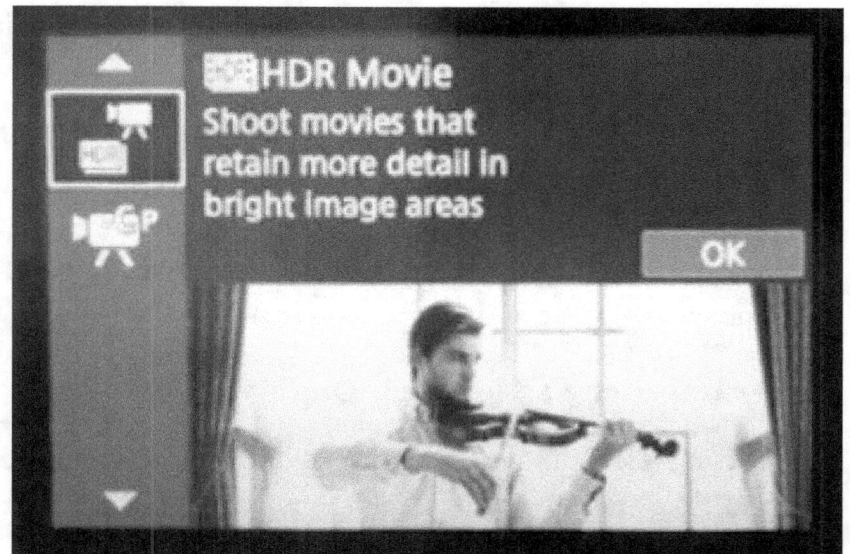

To utilize HDR shooting, follow these steps:

1. **Enable HDR Shooting**

   Start by accessing your camera's settings and enabling the HDR shooting mode. This mode may be found in the video settings or general shooting settings, depending on the camera model.

2. **Select the Right Movie Settings**

   Once HDR shooting is enabled, it's important to choose the appropriate movie settings for your specific shooting conditions. Consider factors such as frame rate, resolution, and any other video-related settings that align with your creative vision.

3. Press Q/SET Button to Enable HDR Movie Shooting

After configuring the movie settings, press the designated button (often labeled Q/SET) to activate HDR Movie Shooting. This action instructs the camera to capture multiple frames at different exposure levels to encompass a wider dynamic range.

4. Frame Merging for High-Quality Video

During HDR movie shooting, your camera captures multiple frames of the same scene at varying exposure levels. The camera then merges these frames to create a single video with enhanced details in both bright and dark regions. This process ensures that the final video reflects a more balanced and visually pleasing representation of the scene's dynamic range.

5. Experiment for Best Results

HDR shooting provides an opportunity for experimentation. Try different settings, adjust exposure values, and explore various shooting scenarios to determine the optimal HDR configuration for your specific needs and creative preferences.

6. Be Aware of Possible Noise or Distortion

While HDR shooting significantly improves the dynamic range, it's essential to be mindful of potential side effects, such as increased noise or distortion.

Experimenting with different settings will help strike a balance between capturing a wide dynamic range and maintaining video quality.

Tips for Shooting Better Video

You probably got your Canon EOS R50 mainly for taking photos, but it's good for shooting videos, too. Mirrorless cameras like this one have advanced video features, and some movies are even filmed with similar Canon cameras. Canon also has professional video cameras, like the EOS C70, which can take photos. They use the same lenses and look similar to regular cameras.

Zooming and Video

When taking pictures, a zoom lens's important factors are how wide it can open (aperture), how much it can zoom, and how sharp it is in different settings. You also need to think about lens speed and zoom range for videos. While sharpness is still crucial, it doesn't need to be as perfect because video frames change rapidly, and our eyes don't catch every detail as they do in still photos.

Here are the things left to think about:

- **Zoom lens maximum aperture:** A lens's speed is important for several reasons. A zoom lens with a big opening lets you take photos in dim light, and a wide aperture allows you to control the focus area. Just remember, the light the lens lets in might change as you zoom. If you prefer consistent focus, choosing a lens that maintains the same brightness is good, especially when shooting at different zoom levels.

If you want consistent light in different zoom settings, go for a lens with a fixed aperture, like the Canon L lenses. Cheaper lenses may have varying apertures, like the RF 24-105mm f/4L, where the aperture stays f/4 across the zoom range.

- **Zoom range:** Don't use Zoom too often when filming unless it's for something like a kung-fu movie. However, there are good reasons to use Zoom, especially for long shots going from really wide to super close or the other way around. Usually, you'll use zoom to change the camera's perspective between shots, and having a longer zoom range can save you from constantly moving around. It's also handy for adjusting focus and making the distance between objects look different. Having a longer zoom range gives you more options.

- **Linearity:** Using different lenses on your camera can cause issues when shooting videos. Some lenses may not give you a smooth zoom, leading to jumps or uneven changes in focus. It's crucial to be aware of this if you intend to zoom while recording, especially if your lens doesn't offer a smooth and linear zoom. Lenses designed for cinema use typically provide linear zooming and focus, making them better for certain video effects like changing focus during a shot.

Keep Things Stable and on the Level

Shaky cameras are a problem in photos but are even more troublesome in videos. Canon lenses with image stabilization can help reduce this issue, making them a great choice for handheld video shooting. However, remember that while stabilized shots are perfect for a documentary or a video with a home movie style, they might be distracting or annoying in other situations. Even with image stabilization, excessive camera movement can still be a distraction, regardless of any blurriness in the subject.

To make your videos look more professional, use a tripod for smoother and steadier shots. It helps when combining footage from different angles or times. Avoid switching between tripod and handheld shots to maintain a smooth transition. Tripods are crucial for longer focal lengths, minimizing camera shake, and for various camera movements, enhancing the overall quality of your videos.

Shooting Script

A shooting script is like a detailed plan for your video. It includes what shots you want, the dialogue, sound effects, transitions, and graphics. Even though you can make changes while filming, having a plan helps you know where you're going and how you want to get there.

When making your shooting plan, include many different shots, even if you don't think you'll use them all. Avoid having only long, boring shots – mix them with various views, angles, and perspectives. If you're working on a documentary where the story isn't fully planned, be flexible with your shooting script. Documentaries often evolve during filming and come together in the editing process.

Storyboards

A storyboard is like a visual plan for a movie. It consists of simple drawings in panels that show how each scene should look. You don't need to be an artist; even stick figures are okay. The storyboard helps you see where things should be in each scene, like actors, props, and furniture. It also shows how you want to take pictures or set up shots. You can even use still photos to create a storyboard.

Here are components of a storyboard:

- **Simple Drawings in Panels:** Storyboards typically consist of a series of rectangular panels, each representing a key moment or shot in a scene. Within these panels, simple drawings or sketches are used to illustrate the visual elements and actions taking place.

- **Visualization of Scene Elements:** The primary purpose of a storyboard is to help filmmakers envision the placement of elements within a scene. This includes the positioning of actors, placement of props, and arrangement of furniture or set pieces. The visual representation allows for a clear understanding of spatial relationships and composition.

- **No Artistic Expertise Required:** Importantly, a storyboard is a functional tool rather than a work of art. Filmmakers need not be skilled artists to create a meaningful storyboard. The emphasis is on conveying the essential details and visual concepts to facilitate communication and planning.

- **Guidance for Shots and Camera Angles:** Beyond scene elements, storyboards guide the filmmaker in planning shots and camera angles. They help determine the framing, perspective, and sequencing of shots, providing a roadmap for the cinematography and visual storytelling.

- **Use of Still Photos:** In addition to hand-drawn illustrations, still photos can be incorporated into a storyboard to enhance clarity. These photos can be placeholders for specific shots or scenes, offering a more realistic depiction of the intended visual style.

Storytelling in Video

Today's viewers prefer quick and engaging videos. When creating content, think of video storytelling as a shortcut compared to the slower pace of print media. Keep audio and video focused on advancing the story, allowing the camera to linger only for a compelling reason and briefly.

Remember, seek movement in your scenes. Unlike still photos, movies thrive on showcasing action. For instance, instead of capturing a static image of an old castle in Segovia, Spain, include dynamic elements like a hang glider soaring overhead.

This juxtaposition of old and new adds an interesting contrast to the video, making it more captivating. Avoid creating travel videos resembling slideshow; incorporating motion breathes life into otherwise static scenes.

Use different camera views and angles in your video to keep it interesting. For instance, even though your model shoot may have many close-ups and interviews, including a quick shot of the studio, it sets the scene. Change camera angles regularly while shooting, and stick to simple transitions like quick cuts when editing. Avoid fancy transitions like wipes or dissolves, as they can make your video seem slow to viewers.

Composition

When making movies, there are specific rules and limitations for framing scenes that are different from taking still photos. While some composition principles still apply, there are unique factors to consider in movie shooting.

- **Horizontal compositions only:** Some things, like people and tall buildings, look better in upright pictures. However, movies are always shown in wide, horizontal frames. So, when talking to a tall person, it can be hard to fit them into the frame without cutting off parts. Even if you try creative angles like shooting from the ground, it doesn't always solve the problem perfectly.

- **Wasted space at the sides:** If you want to focus on the full-length figure, moving in might force you to leave a lot of space on the sides. To avoid that, you can get creative or zoom in tightly, sacrificing some of the height in your composition. This way, you use less image area on the sides and keep the main subject prominent.

- **Seamless (or seamed) transitions:** Each picture can tell its own story in photos. However, in movies, each scene must connect with the one before and after. It might seem strange if there's a sudden shift from a wide shot to a close-up unless you're intentionally being creative. Another mistake is the "jump cut," where consecutive shots look very similar, making it seem like the main subject moved abruptly. To avoid this, changing the camera angle by at least 30 degrees between shots is generally recommended unless you intentionally want your images to break the usual rules and look unconventional.

- **The time dimension:** Unlike photos, movies rely on a sequence of images to tell a story. Dull videos result from using fixed shots with a stationary camera. Professional videos often use various camera angles and positions, but you can create quality content even with one camera and good planning.

CONCLUSION

The Canon EOS R50 is more than just a camera; it's a gateway to unleashing your photographic potential. This guide has equipped you with the knowledge and tools to navigate its features, master its techniques, and capture stunning images that reflect your unique vision.

From exploring the intuitive interface to mastering advanced functionalities like autofocus modes and creative control options, you've learned to bend light and capture moments in ways that move and inspire. Remember, the journey of photography is a continuous exploration, and this guide is just the beginning.

www.ingramcontent.com/pod-product-compliance
Lightning Source LLC
Chambersburg PA
CBHW071206290526
45796CB00008B/165